I0805939

Playful STEAM Learning in the Early Years

An Educator's Guide to Screen-Free Explorations

Amanda Sullivan and Amanda Strawhacker

Foreword by Merredith Portsmore

Teachers College Press
Teachers College, Columbia University

Published by Teachers College Press,® 1234 Amsterdam Avenue, New York, NY 10027

Front cover design by Holly Grundon / BHG Graphics. Photo by Freepik.

Library of Congress Cataloging-in-Publication Data is available at loc.gov

ISBN 978-0-8077-8708-3 (paper)
ISBN 978-0-8077-8709-0 (hardcover)
ISBN 978-0-8077-8307-8 (ebook)

Printed on acid-free paper
Manufactured in the United States of America

EARLY CHILDHOOD EDUCATION SERIES

NANCY FILE & CHRISTOPHER P. BROWN, **EDITORS**

Playful STEAM Learning in the Early Years: An Educator's Guide to Screen-Free Explorations
AMANDA SULLIVAN & AMANDA STRAWHACKER

Culturally Responsive Teaching for Infants and Toddlers: Strategies to Strengthen Development and Learning
MARIE L. MASTERSON

Beyond Compliance in Early Childhood Education: Centering Disability, Freedom, and Belonging
MAGGIE BENEKE & HAILEY R. LOVE, EDS.

Addressing Stress With Self-Compassion: A Guide for Early Childhood Teachers
DAVID P. BARRY

Teacher Well-Being in Early Childhood: A Resource for Early Care and Education Professionals
ANGELA C. BAUM & KERRIE L. SCHNAKE

Pro-Blackness in Early Childhood Education: Diversifying Curriculum and Pedagogy in K–3 Classrooms
GLORIA SWINDLER BOUTTE, JARVAIS J. JACKSON, SAUDAH N. COLLINS, JANICE R. BAINES, ANTHONY BROUGHTON, & GEORGE LEE JOHNSON

Seven Crucial Conversations in Early Childhood Education: Where Have We Been and Why Does It Matter?
NANCY FILE, NANCY E. BARBOUR, & ANDREW J. STREMMEL, EDS.

Supporting Korean American Children in Early Childhood Education: Perspectives From Mother-Educators
SOPHIA HAN, JINHEE KIM, SOHYUN MEACHAM, & SU-JEONG WEE

Relationship-Based Care for Infants and Toddlers: Fostering Early Learning and Development Through Responsive Practice
SUSAN L. RECCHIA, MINSUN SHIN, & ELENI LOIZOU

Infants and Toddlers at Work: Using Reggio-Inspired Materials to Support Brain Development, Second Edition
ANN LEWIN-BENHAM

Leading Anti-Bias Early Childhood Programs: A Guide to Change, for Change, 2nd Ed.
LOUISE DERMAN-SPARKS, DEBBIE LEEKEENAN, & JOHN NIMMO

We Are the Change We Seek: Advancing Racial Justice in Early Care and Education
IHEOMA U. IRUKA, TONIA R. DURDEN, KERRY-ANN ESCAYG, & STEPHANIE M. CURENTON

Young Investigators: The Project Approach in the Early Years, 4th Ed.
JUDY HARRIS HELM, LILIAN G. KATZ, & REBECCA WILSON

Emotionally Responsive Teaching: Expanding Trauma-Informed Practice With Young Children
TRAVIS WRIGHT

Rooted in Belonging: Critical Place-Based Learning in Early Childhood and Elementary Teacher Education
MELISSA SHERFINSKI WITH SHARON HAYES

Transforming Early Years Policy in the U.S.: A Call to Action
MARK K. NAGASAWA, LACEY PETERS, MARIANNE N. BLOCH, & BETH BLUE SWADENER, EDS.

Music Therapy With Preschool Children on the Autism Spectrum: Moments of Meeting
GEOFF BARNES

On Being and Well-Being in Infant/Toddler Care and Education: Life Stories From Baby Rooms
MARY BENSON MCMULLEN

Principals as Early Learning Leaders: Effectively Supporting Our Youngest Learners
JULIE NICHOLSON, HELEN MANIATES, SERENE YEE, THOMAS WILLIAMS JR., VERONICA UFOEGBUNE, & RAUL ERAZO-CHAVEZ

Resisting the Kinder-Race: Restoring Joy to Early Learning
CHRISTOPHER P. BROWN

Reshaping Universal Preschool: Critical Perspectives on Power and Policy
LUCINDA GRACE HEIMER & ANN ELIZABETH RAMMINGER, WITH KATHERINE K. DELANEY, SARAH GALANTER-GUZIEWSKI, LACEY PETERS, & KRISTIN WHYTE

Pre-K Stories: Playing with Authorship and Integrating Curriculum in Early Childhood
DANA FRANTZ BENTLEY & MARIANA SOUTO-MANNING

Ready or Not: Early Care and Education's Leadership Choices—12 Years Later, 2nd Ed.
STACIE G. GOFFIN & VALORA WASHINGTON

For a complete list of series titles, visit https://www.tcpress.com/ece

continued

Early Childhood Education Series, *continued*

Teaching STEM in the Preschool Classroom
ALISSA A. LANGE ET AL.

High-Quality Early Learning for a Changing World
BEVERLY FALK

Guiding Principles for the New Early Childhood Professional
VALORA WASHINGTON & BRENDA GADSON

Leading for Change in Early Care and Education
ANNE L. DOUGLASS

When Pre-K Comes to School
BETHANY WILINSKI

Continuity in Children's Worlds
MELISSA M. JOZWIAK ET AL.

The Early Intervention Guidebook for Families and Professionals, 2nd Ed.
BONNIE KEILTY

STEM Learning with Young Children
SHELLY COUNSELL ET AL.

Courageous Leadership in Early Childhood Education
SUSI LONG ET AL., EDS.

Teaching Kindergarten
JULIE DIAMOND ET AL., EDS.

The New Early Childhood Professional
VALORA WASHINGTON ET AL.

Teaching and Learning in a Diverse World, 4th Ed.
PATRICIA G. RAMSEY

In the Spirit of the Studio, 2nd Ed.
LELLA GANDINI ET AL., EDS.

Exploring Mathematics Through Play in the Early Childhood Classroom
AMY NOELLE PARKS

Becoming Young Thinkers
JUDY HARRIS HELM

The Early Years Matter
MARILOU HYSON & HEATHER BIGGAR TOMLINSON

Thinking Critically About Environments for Young Children
LISA P. KUH, ED.

Standing Up for Something Every Day
BEATRICE S. FENNIMORE

FirstSchool
SHARON RITCHIE & LAURA GUTMANN, EDS.

Early Childhood Education for a New Era
STACIE G. GOFFIN

Everyday Artists
DANA FRANTZ BENTLEY

Multicultural Teaching in the Early Childhood Classroom
MARIANA SOUTO-MANNING

Inclusion in the Early Childhood Classroom
SUSAN L. RECCHIA & YOON-JOO LEE

Moral Classrooms, Moral Children, 2nd Ed.
RHETA DEVRIES & BETTY ZAN

Defending Childhood
BEVERLY FALK, ED.

Starting with Their Strengths
DEBORAH C. LICKEY & DENISE J. POWERS

The Play's the Thing
ELIZABETH JONES & GRETCHEN REYNOLDS

Twelve Best Practices for Early Childhood Education
ANN LEWIN-BENHAM

Big Science for Growing Minds
JACQUELINE GRENNON BROOKS

What If All the Kids Are White? 2nd Ed.
LOUISE DERMAN-SPARKS & PATRICIA G. RAMSEY

Seen and Heard
ELLEN LYNN HALL & JENNIFER KOFKIN RUDKIN

Connecting Emergent Curriculum and Standards in the Early Childhood Classroom
SYDNEY L. SCHWARTZ & SHERRY M. COPELAND

Infants and Toddlers at Work
ANN LEWIN-BENHAM

Educating and Caring for Very Young Children, 2nd Ed.
DORIS BERGEN ET AL.

Beginning School
RICHARD M. CLIFFORD & GISELE M. CRAWFORD, EDS.

Emergent Curriculum in the Primary Classroom
CAROL ANNE WIEN, ED.

Enthusiastic and Engaged Learners
MARILOU HYSON

Powerful Children
ANN LEWIN-BENHAM

Supervision in Early Childhood Education, 3rd Ed.
JOSEPH J. CARUSO WITH M. TEMPLE FAWCETT

Guiding Children's Behavior
EILEEN S. FLICKER & JANET ANDRON HOFFMAN

The War Play Dilemma, 2nd Ed.
DIANE E. LEVIN & NANCY CARLSSON-PAIGE

Playing to Get Smart
ELIZABETH JONES & RENATTA M. COOPER

The Emotional Development of Young Children, 2nd Ed.
MARILOU HYSON

Young Children Continue to Reinvent Arithmetic—2nd Grade, 2nd Ed.
CONSTANCE KAMII

Bringing Learning to Life
LOUISE BOYD CADWELL

Bringing Reggio Emilia Home
LOUISE BOYD CADWELL

Contents

Foreword

The future of our world depends on how well we prepare today's youth to think critically and solve the complex challenges of tomorrow. We frequently hear about science, technology, engineering, arts, and mathematics—collectively known as STEAM—in the field of education. As the world becomes increasingly reliant on advancements in science and engineering, it's clear why today's youth need a strong foundation in these subjects. However, it's not enough for them to simply acquire knowledge in these areas; the challenges of the modern world demand that they become innovative thinkers and problem-solvers.

Today's youth are tomorrow's voters on crucial issues like clean water, renewable energy, and cybersecurity. They may also become the scientists and engineers tackling problems like sustainable energy, access to clean water, and personalized medicine. Across the board, we also know that technology, innovation, and policy need to be considered through the lens of equity, inclusion, and accessibility to reduce harm and expand the help these advancements can afford to more people.

But simply telling youth about STEAM from preschool through high school isn't enough to develop the thinking and problem-solving skills they'll need. They must be engaged in hands-on challenges that give them the chance to innovate, evaluate, and explore ideas. They need opportunities to try and fail, to discuss and compare, and to have safe spaces to engage with STEAM materials and concepts. *How* they learn STEAM is just as important as *what* they learn.

Creating these learning experiences is no easy feat, particularly for young learners. In addition, while technology has its time and place, educators and families also want options for screen-free play and learning. This is exactly the challenge that Dr. Amanda Sullivan and Dr. Amanda Strawhacker have tackled with this book.

I have had the pleasure of knowing Dr. Sullivan and Dr. Strawhacker for several years through my role as director of the Tufts Center for Engineering Education and Outreach. Both bring an impressive blend of cutting-edge research expertise and practical experience as educators. They are just as comfortable synthesizing complex data and theory as they are sitting on the floor with pipe cleaners, construction paper, and a group of children.

They've played pivotal roles in projects involving innovative technologies like ScratchJr, KIBO, and translating CRISPR gene-editing for young learners. There is no better pair to translate their deep experience and research into creative, accessible, and developmentally appropriate practices that any educator can adopt.

At the heart of their work—and this book—is play. You might not think of play and learning together, or believe that play is what will solve the challenges facing our world. However, play and playful learning are exactly what is needed to foster the kind of thinking and problem-solving skills we need today's youth to develop. Play is creative, meaningful, and social. It allows youth to try out and iterate on their own new ideas in a safe space and to consider how their actions and constructions impact the world around them. In this book, the Amandas provide screen-free ways to engage young learners with engineering, science, makerspaces, coding, and more—all through play. From a STEAM dramatic play area to coding a robot without a computer, they synthesize playful, screen-free experiences for educators.

At the heart of my center's mission is the goal of nurturing the next generation of innovators. This book is a powerful tool in advancing that mission. With its playful, screen-free STEAM activities and practical frameworks, it empowers educators to transform their classrooms into vibrant hubs of creativity, innovation, and discovery—whether they're just beginning their STEAM journey or are seasoned experts ready to take their teaching to the next level.

Merredith Portsmore
Director
Research Associate Professor
Center for Engineering Education and Outreach
Tufts University

Acknowledgments

We would like to thank our mentor Dr. Marina Umaschi Bers for her guidance, encouragement, and support over the years. None of our work in this field would be possible without you and the amazing team at the DevTech Research Group. Thank you for opening our eyes to the world of possibilities when it comes to unplugged and screen-free computer science and computational thinking!

We would also like to thank Dr. Merredith Portsmore for supporting this project and generously writing a foreword to this book. We have both learned so much about playful learning in STEAM from our experiences with you and the researchers at the Center for Engineering Education and Outreach at Tufts University.

Thank you to our editor, Sarah Jubar, for believing in this work from the very beginning and encouraging us to pursue this project. You have been with Amanda Sullivan since her *Breaking the STEM Stereotype* days and supported Amanda Strawhacker through her first academic book. Now, neither of us can imagine working with any other editor!

We also want to thank the dozens of schools, hundreds of teachers, and thousands of children who have helped us grow as researchers, educators, and caregivers, and shaped over a decade of our work in child development, which culminates in this book. We are so grateful for all the learning you have shared.

Amanda Sullivan would like to thank her whole family for their unwavering love and support throughout this project. Thank you, Adam, for always being ready to let me bounce ideas off of you, edit chapters, and to motivate me. Thank you to my kitty, Larson, for staying up and cuddling me through all the late nights and early mornings writing. Thank you from the bottom of my heart to my two little scientists, Sidney and Sienna, for being my inspiration for all things—especially all things Playful STEAM. There is no one I would rather build, experiment, and explore with than you two. Thank you to my lifelong friends Safiya and Katie for always supporting and encouraging me, personally and professionally. Thank you to all my friends and colleagues from NGCP, DevTech, Tufts, and elsewhere who have encouraged and supported me. I also want to thank all my nieces and nephews and all the children and educators I have had the honor of working with over the years. Thank you for reminding me about the value of joy, laughter, play, and FUN in learning. Last but not least, thank you to my incredible coauthor, forever work wife, and friend, Amanda Strawhacker. I could not have done this with anyone else. Thank you for making this book so much fun to write. I'm looking forward to whatever our next collaboration will be!

Amanda Strawhacker would like to gratefully acknowledge her entire family for the enduring support throughout the writing of this book, from child care to motivational chats to proofreads and more. Thank you to my mom, who originally suggested we author this book over a decade ago and has graciously listened to every status update and roadblock that arose throughout the actual writing process. Thank you, Jeff, for your unwavering faith in me and unquestioning support in my pursuit of this and all my professional achievements. Thank you to our dog, Otis, who kept this author's feet warm and snuggly through many chilly writing days on the couch. A huge hug, kiss, and forever thank you to my playmate and research partner, my daughter June, who teaches me to be curious, stay silly, and find new ways to play and wonder every day. Thank you so much to all the friends and colleagues who encouraged me along the way with discussions about cognition and learning, and the many, many friends who have become amazing aunties, uncles, and parents and shared their invaluable perspectives on the ways children play. They say it takes a village to raise a child—and also to write a book about them! Finally, thank you to my coauthor. Amanda, I love to converse with you off-screen and through the writing process together. You inspire me to strive as an investigator and changemaker, and I'm so grateful to have you as a work wife and partner in all our passion projects.

What STE(A)M Is and Why It Matters

"Just go outside and play" is something the two of us heard a lot while growing up. Perhaps you grew up with adults telling you the same thing. This open-ended directive to go outside and play without any guidelines, restrictions, or step-by-step instructions allowed us to find creative ways to fill our childhood boredom. To use our imaginations. To dream and discover new things about the familiar places in our neighborhoods. And in fact, it also allowed us to engage with science and engineering. Whether it was building tall sandcastles on the beach and observing geckos in the grass on Oahu (Amanda Sullivan) or getting lost in the woods exploring creeks and animal tracks in Delaware (Amanda Strawhacker), our play experiences allowed us to test hypotheses and learn about the world around us.

Think of children today. They may still hear "go outside and play" as we did in generations past. We hope that they still go outside and make discoveries about the natural environment they are growing up in. But things have gotten a bit more complicated. The environment young children are growing up in today is filled with electronic devices and automated technologies as much as it is filled with grass, sand, and trees. For the first time, unlike any generations before, children today are immersed in an environment full of "smart" technologies.

In today's tech-rich environment, what is the equivalent of telling a child to just go outside and play? It might be to just play a game on a tablet, video console, computer, or to watch television. Children may do this with child safety settings on and have very little step-by-step guidance or supervision from an adult. But even though an adult isn't guiding this experience, the games and activities that children encounter on devices are not the same as open-ended real-world experiences. Most games, apps, and digital products for children are very structured, engaging them more as passive observers than active directors of their own play. This is not an accurate parallel to a child using their imagination to spontaneously play and explore in the natural world. Children may be *engaged* with technology and media, but they are not learning how technology and media *actually work*. They are consumers of their digital experience rather than creators of it.

This is where STEAM (science, technology, engineering, arts, and mathematics) comes in, and particularly the "T" of technology and "E" of engineering. Dale Dougherty, MIT professor and founder of the maker movement, recognized the creative and experimental potential of technology and engineering when he wrote that "new technologies present an invitation to play [and] makers are enthusiasts who play with technology to learn about it. Makers give it a try; they take things apart; and they try to do things that even the manufacturer did not think of doing" (Dougherty, 2013, p. 7). Like other scholars on playful learning (e.g., Piaget, 1973), Dougherty argues that as educators, we should help children use technology to build and craft their *own* tools, solve their own problems, and explore their own questions, rather than completing puzzles or tasks simply because they've been directed to, or to prove that they can. Integrated STEAM learning, with its emphasis on design through building, coding, and crafting, invites connections across its constituent domains to allow for flexible, learner-led creation. This makes STEAM the perfect context in which to explore *how* human-made artifacts and technologies work, and also to understand and experiment with *why* we apply them to certain designs, situations, and challenges. Technology, like any tool, can empower the learner to engage their full creative power and ability—or it can be an expensive babysitter, depending on how it's used. STEAM play, coding, and computational thinking are the processes that allow children to invent and create with new technology, turning a technological object into a tool for learning and thinking.

WHY THIS BOOK?

We were inspired to tackle this complicated issue of how to effectively turn technology into a learning tool, as well as related questions around screen time, STEAM integration, and 21st-century digital skills, based on our own experiences as researchers, educators, and mothers. We know firsthand how complicated it is to follow the wave of changing technologies, keep up with ever-evolving curricular frameworks around coding and computational thinking, and interpret inconsistent guidelines about screen time exposure. Believe us when we tell you that we struggle with these same issues in our own classroom settings and homes with our children. Our goal for this book is to show parents, educators, caregivers, and other practitioners working with young children that it *is* possible to offer young children playful, hands-on, sensory-rich introductions to traditionally "high-tech" STEAM concepts such as coding and computational thinking without relying solely on screen-based technologies and apps.

Although in this book we advocate for unplugged approaches with young children, we are by no means Luddites or technophobes. In fact, we each spent most of our careers on the development of innovative digital technologies and games for young children working with the Developmental Technologies ("DevTech") Research Group at Tufts University (relocated to Boston College as of the writing of this book). But we also know that digital technology is not the only way to go. For reasons we will discuss in this book around cost, equity, and screen time, we believe it is important to develop and disseminate research-backed approaches to teaching STEAM concepts that do not rely heavily on expensive tech tools or Internet access. In this book, we are bringing our decades of experience in the educational technology world and translating it into unplugged, playful, and screen-free opportunities for children to learn and make discoveries. When we choose to present digital technologies throughout this book, we hope to help shift readers' mindsets of what "technology" can and should look like. While we might immediately picture kids sitting alone on computers or iPads with headphones on working silently, by the end of this book we hope to shift this image to a collaborative, hands-on scene, using screen-free tangible technologies that allow for play and movement.

In this book, we take an interdisciplinary STEAM approach to teaching technology and engineering concepts because we truly believe in the power of the arts. Each of us brings our background and passion for the arts to this book, Amanda Sullivan with her love of the performing arts and experience as a former elementary school drama teacher who now integrates the dramatic arts into STEAM curricula and Amanda Strawhacker with her lifelong experience as an avid music lover and performer, a mentor for student musicians, and eventually a researcher exploring how children apply creativity and design to musical exploration. Together, we have sought ways to expand our interest in STEAM into educational outreach, leading independent "STEAM Saturday" classes at public schools in our local community for children to explore STEM (science, technology, engineering, mathematics) concepts in a playful, unstructured environment (more on this in Chapter 7). We have also grown our understanding of the "arts" beyond performance and fine arts to include the liberal arts, civics, history, humanities, and more. In our own teaching work, we have seen firsthand that by incorporating the arts and engaging children in real-world questions using a playful, integrated STEAM approach, we are able to reach a wider range of students, and not just those who are already interested in and confident about STEM. If our goal is to promote equity and diversity across the sciences and technical fields, we know that we must reach *all* young learners and show them the ways they can (and often already do) identify and relate to the sciences. We must strive to break STEM stereotypes by showing the creative, collaborative, and artistic sides that exist in the sciences and engineering.

Finally, we also come to this book as researchers, trained with doctorate-level knowledge of current issues and evidence in areas of human development, child study, and technology-mediated education. Research seems to confirm our personal belief and experience that young children can benefit cognitively, emotionally, and even socially from a playful, screen-free introduction to 21st-century concepts such as coding, computer science, and engineering, which were formerly believed to be too advanced and technical for early childhood (e.g., Bers, 2008; Clements, 1999; Fessakis et al., 2013; Metz, 2007; Papadakis & Kalogiannakis, 2022). This book will summarize these findings in a digestible way and share evidence-based ways that early childhood education professionals and caregivers can implement developmentally appropriate screen-free and low-tech STEAM education with toddlers, young children, and early elementary students. Through practical suggestions, illustrative vignettes, and convincing research summaries, this book aims to shift the mindset of what STEAM learning looks like at an early age and present the many benefits of a playful, screen-free approach to early learning of technical concepts.

THE POWER OF PLAY

At the heart of it all, we are writing this book because we firmly believe in learning through play. Play was an important and memorable part of both of our childhoods and the childhood experiences we are fostering with our own children and students. And yet play is slowly disappearing for many children. Open-ended time to "just go play" as we experienced growing up has slowly been displaced by a focus on teaching academic skills through direct instruction (Hirsh-Pasek et al., 2009; Nicolopoulou, 2010). This emphasis on more academic and content-based approaches to preschool and kindergarten education comes at the expense of more child-centered, play-oriented, and constructivist and constructionist approaches (Hirsh-Pasek et al., 2009; Miller & Almon, 2009; Nicolopoulou, 2010; Papert, 1990).

As educators in the field of early childhood development, this breaks our hearts. It's very hard to overstate the importance of play for all areas of development, but we also know that play is the best and most natural way for young children to learn academic skills. Ginsburg (2007) identifies play as:

> [critical for children's] imagination, dexterity, and physical, cognitive, and emotional strength, [and] important for healthy brain development. [. . .] Play allows children to create and explore a world they can master, conquering their fears while practicing adult roles; [. . .]; develop new competencies that lead to enhanced confidence and the resiliency they will need to face future challenges; [and] learn how to work in groups, to share, to negotiate, to resolve conflicts, and to learn self-advocacy skills. [. . .] Perhaps above all, play is a simple joy that is a cherished part of childhood. (Ginsburg, 2007, p. 183)

In the context of STEAM education, play leads to improved academic and social outcomes by allowing children to build strategies and dispositions for lifelong learning (Hirsh-Pasek et al., 2009). In science, for example, the most important scientific concept or skill that a toddler or young child can learn is a curiosity and joy for the sciences. Throughout this book, we focus on playful strategies that will keep children engaged and in the lead as the directors of their own learning. But more than that, we hope that the activities and strategies in the book will keep children laughing, having fun, and playing alongside their adults.

STEAM IN EARLY CHILDHOOD

Early childhood STEAM education has historically focused on building foundational numeracy skills and an understanding of the natural sciences for young children (Bers, 2008; Bers et al., 2013; Moomaw & Davis, 2010). Educators may have noticed that in the 21st century, STEM education has been slowly replaced by "STEAM," which refers to learning that integrates science, technology, engineering, *arts*, and mathematics (Boy, 2013). This newer acronym is meant to convey the promotion of creativity and expression through technology and science, and is growing in popularity across the United States and worldwide (Allen-Handy et al., 2020; Watson, 2020; Yakman, 2008). In this book, we take the position that arts can be broadly interpreted to mean any approach that brings interpretive, expressive, and humanistic perspectives to STEM activities. This might involve concepts from disciplines like civics and history, language and literacy, ethics and philosophy, and the whole range of liberal arts. This expansion of what qualifies as STEAM is not meant to diminish the rigor of traditional STEM disciplines, but rather to highlight that we use tools of science, engineering, technology, and math in service of solving broad and socially situated human problems. What is the point of educating a master builder who does not have the compassion to understand why a community might need a bridge?

In early childhood, integrated educational STEAM experiences offer inclusive spaces for both children and educators. STEAM lets children explore diverse approaches, perspectives, and representations within STEM, allowing for a more nuanced personal identification with STEM domains (Strawhacker & Sullivan, 2021). Because STEAM offers the flexibility and open-endedness inherent in arts pedagogies (Robelen, 2011), this approach addresses the common argument from critics of technology-mediated education that early exposure to computers may inhibit children's natural play and creativity (e.g., Cordes & Miller, 2000; Oppenheimer, 2003). The arts also help educators engage more richly with STEM. Research shows that while preservice and inservice early childhood educators around the world are often insecure about their own STEM skills and hesitant to introduce STEM to their students (e.g., Dong & Xu, 2021; Masoumi, 2020), teachers show much more confidence and comfort with arts integration (Bresler, 2007; Hartman & Dani, 2020). Incorporating the arts makes STEM more accessible in classrooms by allowing teachers to leverage their experience in arts education to create successful and engaging entry points into STEAM investigations.

STEAM AND THE DIGITAL DIVIDE

When we think of the "T" of technology and "E" of Engineering in STEAM and the curricular topics associated with them, we may think of topics like computer science, coding, computational thinking, and engineering. Now more than ever, robotics kits, phone and tablet apps, websites, and videogames are being marketed specifically at young children in preK–2nd grade. Popular apps like CodeSpark Academy, Kodable, and ScratchJr invite children ages 4 to 8 to code their own animations and games, while robotic kits like Bee-Bot, Cubetto, and Code-a-Pillar are meant to engage children as young as 2 years old in tangible explorations of movement-based coding logic.

Despite the widespread market availability of new digital tools for young children to explore STEAM and learn about their human-engineered environment, many of these resources are prohibitively expensive or technologically complicated for adults to meaningfully implement (Sullivan & Strawhacker, 2021). For example, common commercially available robotics kits that allow children to explore engineering, sensors, coding, and computational thinking run between $200 and $300 per kit, which unfortunately is outside the budget of many early childhood education centers and parents. Even the best free coding applications and videogames require schools or homes to have access to tablets, computers, or other consoles in order for children to use them. In addition to the financial barriers, early childhood educators who are lucky enough to have access to these tools may still require hours of professional development or training to be able to use them appropriately with children in their learning setting. One of the many outcomes of the global COVID-19 pandemic was the spotlight it shone on inequities of Wi-Fi and digital access, with individuals in rural and developing areas hit hardest. As of 2021, the Federal Communications Commission (FCC) reported that 97% of Americans in urban areas had access to a high-speed, fixed Internet service, compared with 65% in rural areas and 60% on tribal lands (Roese, 2021). This trend is echoed on a global scale, with less than half the rate of Internet penetration in developing nations compared to developed ones (Roese, 2021).

This has led to a persistent "digital divide," or a socioeconomic division between those who have access to reliable Internet access and devices with high-quality, open-ended software and technology and those who do not. For example, access to computer science classes and clubs is generally lowest for students from lower-income households (Busteed & Sorenson, 2015). Inequitable access to computer science education could place these students at a disadvantage as computer technology continues to advance, especially as coding is thought of as "the new literacy" in this day and age (Bers, 2018).

As authors, we want to make our stance clear: *There is nothing wrong with using digital technologies, iPad applications, videogames, or other screen-based technologies or media.* As mentioned earlier, we have both worked on the development of various apps, games, websites, and digital technologies for young children, and we stand by their incredible educational potential (at the end of the book, we will provide more information on some of these best tools and strategies for introducing and integrating these screen-based tools into STEAM learning!). But if we are to democratize the 21st-century learning opportunities that technological tools are meant to unlock—computational thinking, design-based innovation and creativity, playful inquiry and curiosity—we must also invest in low-cost, accessible, and inclusive pathways to this kind of learning. That is where unplugged, screen-free STEAM learning comes in and where our Playful STEAM Learning Framework (PSLF) can make the most impact.

It is worth noting that "screen-free" does not always equate to "low-cost." Later in this book, we will be discussing and showcasing some amazing screen-free tools such as robotics and engineering kits that are programmed with tangible interfaces and that are commercially available for use in home, school, and informal education spaces. We believe these tools are worth highlighting to showcase that using digital technology does not always need to mean sitting in front of a computer, tablet, or television. These technologies demonstrate the way the educational technology industry is advancing to meet young children's developmental needs in innovative ways. However, while we believe these tools are important to introduce to parents and educators so that they are able to gain a full picture of what "screen-free STEAM" can look like with young children, we recognize that they are likely cost-prohibitive for most education or home settings. Therefore, the main emphasis throughout most of this book will be on unplugged and hands-on activities that are free or cheap for anyone to implement with young children.

SCREEN TIME

We have talked a lot about screen time up to this point without really digging into what it is and why it is important to consider exposure to it with young children. Unlike unstructured outdoor time, long stretches of unsupervised screen time can have potentially harmful effects on children's developing eyesight, physical activity levels, social interactions, and more (World Health Organization, 2019). Despite this, international trends suggest young children are increasingly using digital technologies, and the age of first use is getting younger (Hooft Graafland, 2018). For example, more than half (52%) of 3–4-year-olds and the majority (82%) of 5–7-year-olds growing up in the United Kingdom are now online, according to caregiver reports (Ofcom, 2020). It's very common for children today to have their first experience with digital technology before the age of 2, when they are likely still in diapers (Chaudron et al., 2019).

Educators (and parents) are often concerned about this increased exposure to digital technologies, and for good reason. For example, the World Health Organization (WHO) and American Academy of Pediatrics (AAP) both recommend avoiding screen time entirely (or limiting to infrequent interactive activities like live video chatting) below age 2 and working toward a limit of 1 hour or less of daily screen time (adult supervised) for children ages 2–5 (Council on Communications and Media, 2016; World Health Organization, 2019). The AAP has also developed the Family Media Use Plan for older kids, which supports parents and children to negotiate limits and boundaries around screen usage.

Certainly, there are valid concerns and reasons for limiting (or completely eliminating) screen time with young children. However, we also know that fostering digital skills at a young age is important so that children can use digital devices effectively and safely as they grow up. If we believe that a goal of equitable STEAM education should be access to the learning that technologies can afford, we must acknowledge that eventually, children should be able to explore technological environments through play. For children to be empowered as citizens in the digitally connected 21st-century world, they must learn not just how to use technology but how to *understand* it, how to recognize the constraints and possibilities of human-made artifacts, and how to use these powerful tools responsibly and for positive impactful change.

We do not advocate sheltering children from experiences in the world, especially ones that can provide such a rich opportunity for engagement and creativity, or that might even be required to fully participate in the global economy that they will inherit. However, we also deeply respect the importance of keeping digital exploration safe, appropriate, and befitting the readiness level of children at different ages and stages of development. How can we prepare children for a world filled with digital environments without unnecessary screen time or expensive equipment? There are so many strategies and approaches that you will explore in this book, but one of the best tools we can offer is the Playful STEAM Learning Framework. This pedagogical tool (and the associated handy mnemonic "PLAY") will help you remember to keep children in the driver's seat of their own learning, infuse everyday experiences with a joy of STEAM discovery, and most importantly, stay playful!

THE PLAYFUL LEARNING STEAM FRAMEWORK

Beginning in Chapter 1 and throughout this book, we will present our Playful STEAM Learning Framework (PSLF) and use it as a guide for developing inclusive, engaging, and educational STEAM experiences for children that build mastery and confidence over time. The PSLF provides parents, caregivers, and educators with exemplary-practice guidelines on how to foster young children's playful STEAM learning with minimal use of screen-based technologies. This framework is rooted in a combination of child-led and adult-scaffolded play experiences. The four main pillars of the PSLF are:

1. **P**ersevering through "hard fun"
2. **L**istening to children's ideas,
3. **A**ctively supporting inclusion, and
4. Saying **Y**es to open-ended sensory play.

We chose to use the acronym **PLAY** to remember these four pillars to remind us that play is at the heart of how young children learn, socialize, and make authentic discoveries. This framework will be described in detail in Chapter 2 and referenced throughout the book in practice examples and pedagogical applications.

SHIFTING MINDSETS

By taking a hands-on and screen-free approach to STEAM in this book, we hope to shift mindsets about what it looks like to explore technology, engineering, and computing with young children. Before we dig deeper, take a moment to check in with yourself and your own beliefs or priorities. In Table I.1, you can read some opinion statements about STEAM education and technology-mediated learning. These statements are not "good" or "bad" but represent perspectives that might change over the course of your own STEAM integration journey. Each statement also has a 1–5 scale next to it, where 1 means "I strongly disagree," 3 means "I neither agree nor disagree," and 5 means "I strongly agree." Read each statement and decide where on the 1 to 5 scale you feel your level of agreement is, and mark your answers to return to later. You can interpret your results below and read what your choices communicate about where you are in your STEAM learning pathway. You may find it helpful to revisit the check-in after reading this book or exploring different screen-free and technology-mediated STEAM

Table I.1. Self-Check-In on Playful STEAM Mindsets and Practices

Statement	1	2	3	4	5
I use screen-based technology regularly with children in my learning/home setting.					
I offer technology to my students/children for more than a time-filler or a reward.					
I have tried introducing computer science and/or engineering to young children.					
I know how to teach computer science and/or engineering to young children.					
I have no problem finding ways to talk about STEM during arts, free play, or other activities.					
I know how to integrate the arts with STEM.					
I believe all my students/children are equally engaged by STEM content in my learning setting.					
I believe my students/children are exposed to diverse and representative STEM role models.					
I provide my students/children with ample opportunities for child-led play.					
I know how to scaffold my students'/children's play to help them make STEM connections.					
1 = strongly disagree, 2 = somewhat disagree, 3 = neither agree or disagree, 4 = somewhat agree, 5 = strongly agree					

activities with children to see if your perspective has changed, and how. This check-in table can also be a helpful tool to share with colleagues or parents of young children to foster discussions around beliefs and practices with technology and STEM in early childhood settings.

If you answered mostly 1–2s on the self-check-in, then we are so glad that this book found its way to you! Exploring STEAM for early childhood might make you feel a bit like a pioneer setting out in the wilderness. Think of this book as your map and compass, offering accessible starting points and goals to help you grow your knowledge and experience with STEAM play. You might find that Parts I and II are especially helpful as you explore new concepts and consider how they might apply to your own learning setting.

If you answered mostly 3s, you might already be familiar with STEAM education, and curious about how to expand your pedagogical tool-belt. The strategies presented in this book may resonate with experiences you've explored or tested, and we hope you find new sources of inspiration to keep your STEAM learning playful, engaging, and child-led. If you're feeling committed to the idea of STEAM integration but looking for ways to keep the learning going, check out Part III. This section emphasizes authentic and organic STEAM experiences—no expensive tools, lengthy curricula, or screen time required!

If you answered mostly 4–5s on the self-check-in, you may already identify as a STEAM education leader in your community or learning setting. We hope you are proud of all you've already accomplished to welcome children into an inclusive and diverse world of STEAM, and we offer this book as a resource with even more ideas to continue fostering a joy of learning! In addition to exploring the many ideas and suggestions for learning tools and activities presented in Part IV, you may find that the children you work with are ready to graduate to more advanced STEAM concepts and technologies. Check out the book's Conclusion for tips about how to scaffold children's first experiences with screen-based technologies.

READY TO LEARN MORE?

Let's dive into what you can expect to discover in this book. Part I explores research evidence around the benefits of screen-free STEAM, exploring the role of play, the power of screen-free computational learning, and questions of how to democratize computational thinking for diverse learners and settings.

In Part II, we shift to thinking about teaching strategies and pedagogical moves to support playful STEAM learning and explore specific considerations for formal classroom and informal out-of-school time spaces.

Part III is where we share real-world practice examples of how playful STEAM learning can emerge in any setting—no screen time or expensive tools required! We'll discuss illustrative examples of STEAM exploration and inquiry, everywhere from daily home and neighborhood settings, to the great outdoors, and during specialized activities like messy making or dramatic play.

After we look closely at low- and no-tech STEAM, Part IV will introduce examples of novel technological tools for learning and ways to introduce children to digital technologies without unnecessary screen time. In addition to considering the technologies that children commonly encounter in daily life, we'll summarize research on how children can learn about coding and computational logic without screen-based technology, and consider ways to seamlessly integrate these concepts into educational settings. Finally, the book concludes with a reflection on how to prepare when children are ready to "graduate" from screen-free to screen-based tools and technologies.

Whether you are hoping to learn about a new-to-you learning domain, incorporate more creativity and intention into your current STEAM teaching practice, or you're already an advocate for playful STEAM learning, we are thrilled that you've chosen this book as part of your own learning journey. We hope you will find, as we have, that when we allow children to take the lead in their own play, they will freely stumble on puzzling questions (or insatiable curiosities!) that lead them down a path rich with scientific investigations, exploratory trials, thoughtful comparisons, measurements, documentation, wondering, building, breaking, testing, refining—all the things that build confidence and competence with STEAM skills! With the framework and research evidence provided in future chapters and colorful examples to spark your thinking, we hope you will be able to use this book as a resource to support playful, welcoming, hands-on, inclusive, messy, and screen-free STEAM learning with the young children in your life—and help them grow a joy of learning and discovery that will inspire them for decades to come!

Part I

WHY SCREEN-FREE STEAM?

CHAPTER 1

STEAM, Play, and Young Children

Almost everyone, from children to adults, knows how to play and how to recognize play when they see it (Pellegrini, 2009; Smith & Vollstedt, 1985), yet somehow, it's one of the most challenging topics for scientists to categorize and define (Burghardt, 2011; Smith et al., 1985; Sutton-Smith, 2009). For example, Stuart Brown, founder of the National Institute for Play, has described play as anything that is spontaneously done for its own sake. It can appear purposeless but usually produces joy and may also lead to mastery of skills (White, 2012).

Part of the challenge of describing play comes from the fact that *any* behavior can be playful, but two people doing the same task are not necessarily both playing (Gray, 2013). How can this be? The reason is that play is not a specific activity but a state of mind, more like a motivation or a mental attitude (Brown & Vaughan, 2009; Gray, 2013). Children's play can be guided or exploratory, social or independent, object-based or imaginative, but all play shares a few key components (Krasnor & Pepler, 1980; Smith & Vollstedt, 1985):

- **Self-motivated:** Play comes from a child's internal impulse for self-satisfaction and has no external purpose or goal.
- **Spontaneous:** Children do not typically have an "end goal" directing their play. The play process can involve repeated iteration or can shift freely throughout a play session.
- **Voluntary:** Children cannot be coerced into playing but must freely choose to engage in play.
- **Active:** Whether mentally or physically, children need to be engaged in the play activity.
- **Fun:** Most importantly, play is pleasurable and enjoyable for the player, creating a feedback loop that spurs continuous engagement in the activity.

Another universal aspect of play is that it is critical for children's early cognitive development and learning (Hirsh-Pasek et al., 2009; Pellegrini, 2009; Scarlett et al., 2004). Neuroscientists now know that children are born with billions of neurons in their brains, but very few of these neurons are connected to each other (Conel, 1939/1967). They need activation from the environment to grow the trillions of neuronal connections that the average adult brain has. Play, or rather the play state of mind, is a natural and instinctive way for children to build those connections, priming the brain to connect pathways across physical, social–emotional, and mental skills. In other words, play literally wires the brain for learning, laying the foundation for lifelong skills of confidence, coping abilities, creativity, and perseverance (Conel, 1939/1967; Hebb, 1949/2005; Liu et al., 2017; White, 2012).

SUPPORTING EARLY LEARNING: ADULT-GUIDED AND CHILD-LED PLAY

Social interaction is an important aspect of learning through play (Nicolopoulou, 1993). Independent free play is a key way for children to spend time working on playful iteration, perseverance, and experimentation. Over time, they learn to be more social and intentional in their play, graduating from solitary and parallel play at 2–3 years to more communicative and collaborative play by ages 3–4 (Parten, 1932). By kindergarten, children are ready for logic-oriented play, such as group activities and rule-based games. Progressing through the stages of play development as identified by Parten (1932) and other scholars may vary for each individual child, and children often appear to be transitioning through multiple stages at once in a single play session. Key milestones as children move through the stages of play development in early childhood might look like:

- **Parallel Play:** This occurs when children play next to each other but are not actually interacting. For example, two children may play with dolls next to each other, but their dollplay does not overlap (Hughes, 2021; Parten, 1932; Scarlett et al., 2004).
- **Associative Play:** During this stage, children begin to be more interested in other children, although they may still primarily play independently. Associative play allows them to begin practicing what they have observed through parallel play to engage with other children or adults during an activity (Hughes, 2021; Parten, 1932; Scarlett et al., 2004).
- **Cooperative Play:** Cooperative play occurs when children engage in play together with the same goal, following agreed-on rules for play and an established division of labor. In order for children to engage in cooperative play, they need to be developmentally able to understand the goals and intentions of another person. Counterintuitively, cooperative play typically involves some interpersonal conflict. This becomes an opportunity for children to explore communication skills, frustration management,

compromise, and negotiation (Parten, 1932; Hughes, 2021; Scarlett et al., 2004).

Adults can support playful learning by scaffolding meaningful connections between play and other familiar aspects of children's lives (Liu et al., 2017). This might look like enriching the child's environment with toys, books, and photographs to promote a specific curricular concept like animals and habitats. Or adults might join children as coplayers and use thoughtful questions and narrative comments to highlight children's discoveries and prompt deeper exploration during play (Fisher et al., 2011).

Both free and guided play are critical in a child-centered approach to learning. Unstructured child-led play allows children true agency to explore their personal questions and impulses, while guided play allows caregivers and educators to target specific learning experiences. In any form, play should always maintain its character as fun, engaging, and intrinsically motivated.

STEAM PLAY MILESTONES

We have established that play is important for early learning and development and that it comes organically and spontaneously to young children. STEAM learning and exploration is also naturally present in young children's play. Each of STEAM's five subject domains (science, technology, engineering, arts, and mathematics) focus on asking questions, making discoveries, creating artifacts, and solving problems. This process of inquiry, discovery, and creation happens every day as young children play and have new experiences. Simply by providing them with materials and opportunities to investigate the world around them—both the natural world and the human-engineered world—adults will stimulate child-directed play and experimentation within STEAM.

Early exposure to STEM (science, technology, engineering, and mathematics) and STEAM (science, technology, engineering, arts, mathematics) is a critical part of early play and learning. Research has demonstrated that children who are exposed to STEM curricula and programming at an early age demonstrate fewer gender-based stereotypes regarding STEM careers, an increased interest in engineering, and fewer obstacles entering these fields later in life (Madill et al., 2007; Markert, 1996; Metz, 2007; Steele, 1997; Sullivan, 2019; Sullivan & Bers, 2017). There are also many cognitive and social benefits from implementing STEAM content, particularly computer science and engineering curricula, with young children (e.g., Bers, 2008; Fessakis et al., 2013; Kazakoff et al., 2013; Lee et al., 2013). For example, some STEAM interventions have been shown to have positive benefits for children's developing numeracy, literacy, and visual memory, and can even prompt collaboration and teamwork (Clements, 1999; Lee et al., 2013).

Table 1.1. Early Childhood STEAM Play Milestones

Age	STEAM Milestones	Play Stages and Transitions	STEAM Play Example
Toddlers (2–3 years)	Sensory exploration Cause and effect Joy of inquiry	Parallel play Associative play	Free exploration of water and sand tables
Preschoolers (4–5 years)	Exploration Observation Hypothesis testing	Associative play Cooperative play	Participating in a nature scavenger hunt
Early Elementary (6–8 years)	Process-based exploration Iteration and revision Problem-solving	Complex imaginative play Rule-based play	Playing a multiplayer STEAM board game such as *Robot Turtles*

Parents and educators often think of STEAM exposure as something that requires a curriculum, lesson planning, expensive materials, and a classroom, library, or lab space to implement. All of these resources are wonderful, but the truth is, positive early experiences with STEAM can also occur naturally through children's self-directed play. Through the conscious addition of some adult scaffolding and support, play is the first (and one of the best) places to begin to support young children's success in STEAM.

The type of playful STEAM experiences adults provide should vary based on a child's age, interests, and specific learning goals. There are some general STEAM play milestones we might expect to see as children develop and progress from the toddler years into preschool and early elementary school (see Table 1.1) (CDC, 2018; Kennedy & Tunnicliffe, 2022). For example, while a STEAM milestone for a young toddler might simply be expressing a joy of exploration through sensory play, a STEAM play milestone for a preschooler might include working with a group to complete a scavenger hunt for natural objects outside. Meanwhile, early elementary school students might be learning new STEAM content by engaging in more structured games such as science-focused board games or card games.

SUPPORTING CHILDREN'S SENSORY STEAM PLAY

When it comes to STEAM play, there are ways for adults to naturally guide and support children's free play in order to spark new connections, discoveries, and "aha!" moments that they might not otherwise reach on their own. At the early childhood level, learning about STEAM often happens first through hands-on play that focuses on sensory exploration. Simply put, sensory play is any form of play that stimulates your senses. Most early childhood educators immediately associate sensory play with "sensory bins" that engage children's sense of touch (e.g., play with water, Play-Doh, kinetic sand, and more). When we think about play that stimulates a broader range of senses, we might expand on these classic sensory play examples to include taste test challenges, balance play like swinging in different ways on a swing, or smelling different kinds of wildflowers on a nature walk.

Although we categorized sensory play as a 2–3-year-old milestone in Table 1.1, this type of play is critical and impactful for children long after it first emerges in toddlerhood. Deans and Wright (2021) note that for young children from age 12 months through 4 years and beyond, learning is based on sensory explorations and relies on active and physical engagement with the world. The beauty of this kind of learning is that most children are naturally drawn to sensory play and find ways to engage in it whether or not adults have intended them to. If you have ever seen toddlers in crisp white clothes jumping in puddles at the park or squishing mud through their fingers to their parents' dismay, you have experienced this firsthand! According to Eisner (2002), the senses are the "first avenues to consciousness." Classic developmentalist Jean Piaget noted that "initial learning" about the world happens through the senses, with initial learning being both reflexive (relying on reflexes such as sucking, flailing arms, shaking head) and reactive (shaking a toy intentionally to make a rattle sound, using language sounds to get certain reactions from a caregiver) (Piaget, 1953, 1969).

Through sensory play, toddlers and young children test hypotheses, make new discoveries, explore cause and effect, and experience new sensations for the first time. Adults can help them make bigger connections during their sensory explorations by offering age-appropriate prompts and asking thought-provoking questions. This kind of support is called *scaffolding*, a term used by child developmentalists to refer to temporary support from an adult that helps a child attain a higher level of skill mastery (Shvarts & Bakker, 2019). Let's use a common sensory play example of making "slime" to illustrate how meaningful adult scaffolding, differentiated by age and developmental stage, can help children make powerful STEAM discoveries.

Playing with slime is a common activity among preschool and early elementary school students. It is easy to see that children love to play by squishing and stretching slime in their hands, but did you know there is a great deal of science behind this exploration? Slime is a non-Newtonian fluid, meaning that it does not follow Newton's law of viscosity (i.e., constant viscosity independent of stress). In non-Newtonian fluids, including slime, viscosity can change when under force, behaving variously like more of a liquid or more of a solid depending on how much pressure is applied to it. How might an educator explain this concept to a young child? The educator might invite the children to explore or imagine stirring pudding with a spoon. When you stir it gently, it feels like a smooth liquid and your spoon goes right in. But if you stir it quickly, it feels thick and harder to move. In other words, non-Newtonian liquids are special because they can act like both a liquid and a solid, depending on how you touch them. This is a perfect example of how hands-on STEAM exploration makes learning concrete and accessible. The concept of "non-Newtonian fluids" seems quite abstract and complicated using only technical definitions and verbal descriptions, but through a hands-on play experience, it can be made understandable and even intuitive to children.

Through slime play, children can explore cause and effect, make and test predictions, explore states of matter, and more. How we support children in their play with slime can be adjusted based on their interests and developmental stages (see Table 1.2). By providing guided prompts and probing

Table 1.2. Free Play Versus Guided Sensory STEAM Play

Age	Free Sensory Play	Guided Sensory Play
Toddlers	Engage students in open-ended sensory play with slime made by an adult.	Engage students in the process of making slime with an adult before playing with it. Encourage students to use their senses to describe the experience (e.g., What does it feel like? What happens when we add a new ingredient?).
Preschoolers	Students follow different slime recipes and explore results.	Encourage students to compare and contrast different slime recipes. Use new vocabulary to describe how the different slime recipes feel, smell, and react. Introduce the term "non-Newtonian fluid" when talking about slime.
Early Elementary	Students invent and compare their own slime recipes and analyze results.	Encourage an exploration of states of matter, including non-Newtonian fluids. Compare Newtonian and non-Newtonian fluids. Help students compare proportions of ingredients and the effect on slime consistency. Encourage documentation of observations through a science notebook or worksheet.

questions, we can take a simple play activity like playing with slime and turn it into deeper STEAM learning. Are you excited to try exploring slime with your own young students? Check out the slime resources, including easy slime recipes, in Appendix A. All appendixes referenced throughout this book are available freely online at https://www.tcpress.com/playful-steam-learning-in-the-early-years-9780807787083.

STEAM PLAY WITH TOYS AND TECH

When it comes to STEM skills, hands-on play with tangible objects is particularly impactful for learning. In fact, kindergarten was originally conceived as a playful context for children to grow and develop in by exploring and experimenting with an assortment of play materials in order to learn about the world around them with minimal adult intervention (Lilley, 1967; Wolfe, 2002). Manipulatives like blocks, sand, balls, crayons, and paper all engage children in learning about physical properties of their environment, laying the groundwork for cause-and-effect logic and visual–spatial awareness (Caldera et al., 1999; Ness & Farenga, 2016; White, 2012). When children engage in free play with tangible toys and manipulatives, they spontaneously use math concepts of counting, measuring, and exploring patterns and shapes (Sarama & Clements, 2009). In one longitudinal study of 37 children, deeper manipulative play in preschool was even linked to improved math and science achievement in high school (Wolfgang et al., 2001).

As mentioned previously, new developmentally appropriate technological softwares and robotic kits have evolved in the tradition of educational manipulatives, and like their predecessors, these tools allow children to explore their understanding of shape and number, spatial relations, and proportion (Brosterman, 1997; Kuh, 2014; Nicholson, 1972; Resnick et al. 1998). Today, there is a growing number of digital devices, robotics kits, videogames, and other digital experiences available to introduce children to computational thinking, computer science, and engineering.

Digital technology *can* be a wonderful way to explore STEAM at the early childhood level. Later in this book, we will look at innovative examples of technologies, such as commercially available robotics kits, for engaging young children in coding and computational thinking. Specifically, we'll introduce tools and approaches that align with this book's pedagogical framework by introducing these concepts through fully tangible interfaces—no screen time required. However, the goal of the book and the framework we present are to demonstrate that expensive technology is not the *only* way to teach coding and engineering to young children. In an attempt to reach all young children, we focus on presenting STEAM activity ideas and materials that are low-cost and easily accessible to all, in order to help bridge the divide in access to computer science and engineering education. A dedication to inclusion and accessibility is at the heart of the book's approach to teaching and learning STEAM in the early years.

SUPPORTING INTELLECTUAL CURIOSITY THROUGH PLAY

All of the types of play described throughout this chapter support children's learning and development across different domains. Perhaps even more importantly, the play we have described supports young children's intellectual curiosity. Intellectual curiosity is the act of asking questions with the purpose of learning something new. Unlike logistical questions about what is for lunch or whether a friend can come over to play, questions that demonstrate intellectual curiosity demonstrate a thirst for understanding the unknown. Anyone who has spent time with young children is familiar with these types of questions, although you may not associate them with intellectual curiosity. These are questions like "why is the sky blue?" and "where do babies come from?" that may at times exasperate early childhood educators and caregivers.

Intellectual curiosity represents an openness to experiences, a desire for novelty, and willingness to embrace the unexpected. When educators help to foster children's intellectual curiosity, they are helping to foster a joy of discovery—a key component in raising lifelong learners. Play, especially STEAM play, provides a very natural opportunity to help foster young children's act of asking questions and to promote their budding intellectual curiosity. Researchers like Dr. Alison Gopnik argue that children start out as little scientists, curious to learn new things about the world around them (Gopnik et al., 1999). At an early age, young learners use deep observations, make predictions, and repeat experiments many times to learn new things about the world around them—strategies as familiar in playrooms and at recess as they are in scientific research labs!

Unfortunately, we have also seen that this scientific inclination and sense of wonder young children have often get stifled once they enter traditional schooling in the United States. Some researchers have estimated that preschool children ask their parents about 100 questions a day, and between ages 2 and 5 kids ask around 40,000 questions (Berger, 2014; Bronson & Merryman, 2010). But there is a steep drop-off after this. At around age 5 (right when many kids are starting formal schooling), the questions they ask drop significantly, from around one question every 2 minutes to less than one question every 2 hours (Engel, 2021). Their curiosity (and their opportunities to play) are often curtailed by the need to cover academic content, the logistics of the school day, and school culture that is more focused on kids providing the *right answers* as opposed to asking the *right questions*.

This is, unfortunately, counterproductive to our goal as early childhood educators.

Curiosity is a driving force behind self-directed learning, and research suggests that fostering intellectual curiosity beginning in kindergarten may be a key determinant of academic success. For example, curiosity has been associated with greater reading and math academic achievement at kindergarten (Shah et al., 2018). Research has also linked curiosity to a number of positive and adaptive behaviors, including tolerance of anxiety and uncertainty, positive emotions, humor, playfulness, out-of-box thinking, and a nonjudgmental attitude (Kashdan et al., 2013).

Recognizing the importance of supporting young children's curiosity through play is nothing new. For decades, researchers have documented the benefits of play to satisfy curiosity and make discoveries. However, shifts in educational policies and priorities that have also emerged in the past two decades have applied pressure to focus on academic goals and high-stakes testing—both of which have resulted in less opportunity for play and more teacher-directed activities (Fung & Cheng, 2012; Lynch, 2015).

CONCLUDING THOUGHTS

Our stance in this book is that when it comes to STEAM learning, playful and hands-on approaches that hone in on children's questions and curiosities will go hand in hand with academic learning and success. Recent research has shown that child-initiated imaginary play and teacher-guided play can promote the science practice, science ideas, and crosscutting concept of patterns needed to explain the phenomenon (Charara et al., 2021). This book aims to support early childhood educators in finding the right balance and strategies for incorporating play as a means to teach STEAM content, with the ultimate goal of creating lifelong, curious learners.

But you may still be wondering: why STEAM? Why integrate these areas instead of exploring each domain separately? In the next chapter, we will answer these questions as we break down the research explaining why an integrated STEAM approach to learning is especially beneficial in the early years. We will introduce the pillars of the Playful STEAM Learning framework and explore why the arts are a critical piece of playful, hands-on learning.

CHAPTER 2

Why Integrate the "A" of the Arts With STEM?

So far in this book, we've discussed the importance of playful, self-guided, sensory exploration to build STEAM skills in the early years; the ability of children to learn STEAM concepts without the aid of screen-based digital tools; and the importance of introducing STEAM concepts and practices early and often to all children, representing the diversity of family backgrounds and individual identities. What educators and caregivers may be wondering now is how to actually achieve this integrated STEAM approach in your specific setting and perhaps why we are even arguing that these disciplines should be integrated in the first place. Isn't it simpler to separate technology from math, or science from the arts, and introduce them to children in a slower and more focused way? This chapter addresses these concerns. Specifically, the chapter emphasizes how integrated education is not just important for early learning but is the most effective way to engage young children in meaningful STEAM exploration. Chapters in Part II of this book will expand on strategies, examples, and benefits of integrated STEAM play in diverse learning settings, from formal school classrooms to at-home explorations, informal after-school programs, and everything in between.

WHY INTEGRATED STEAM IN EARLY CHILDHOOD?

While we argue for the importance of blending the STEAM disciplines in early education, it is important to acknowledge here that we present this argument within a complex terrain of educational, research, policy, and professional perspectives on this integration. It is beyond the scope of this chapter to delve into the broad-spanning history of STEAM as an evolving inter- and transdisciplinary pursuit (for a depth discussion of this topic, we invite readers to review the lovely theoretical discourse outlined by Mejias et al., 2021). However, we will attempt to summarize here what we do *not* mean by STEAM integration and spotlight the emphasis we are placing on real-world multidisciplinary experiences in the context of young children's learning and development.

From a policy perspective, STEAM integration faces a number of challenges to its broad acceptance as an educational movement. In the United States, integrated STEM disciplines have gained traction as a funding buzzword since the 1990s and early 2000s, when researchers argued that U.S. students were losing ground in STEM academic performance compared to students in emerging economies like China and India (Sanders, 2008). Some critics argue that arts advocates arbitrarily infused arts and design into STEAM, taking advantage of the ill-defined boundaries of the disciplines to secure funding for historically marginalized arts education interests (Bequette & Bequette, 2015). Even assuming that STEAM advocates are pursuing well-intentioned goals of infusing creativity, innovation, self-expression, and student agency by lifting the arts in this conversation (e.g., Allina, 2018), STEAM educational initiatives can easily misrepresent or misapply concepts from one or more of its subdisciplines, cherry-picking practices from STEM or the arts and deploying them "in service" of richer initiatives in the other camp (Mejias et al., 2021).

These tensions—which have evolved in the context of economic, nationalistic, and disciplinary-specific histories—are certainly challenging, and we earnestly embrace the call for a "mutually-instrumental and pedagogical" approach to STEAM, in which "the Arts and STEM fields come together, valued and engaged co-equally, specifically in order to advance learning in *both* areas *within and beyond* boundaries" [original emphasis] (Mejias et al., 2021). However, we respectfully hope to move our emphasis in this chapter away from the nascent agendas of world powers and disciplinary authorities, and focus our discussion of STEAM integration within the fine-grained and concrete experiences of young children approaching these multidisciplinary concepts and practices for the very first time.

THE NATURE OF CHILDREN'S LEARNING

What does it mean to accept integrated STEAM as a pedagogical approach for young children, and what does this look like in practice? As you might have guessed from earlier chapters, most effective learning at this age (and, we believe, at any age) comes down to play. Playful, holistic learning experiences naturally incorporate multiple disciplines, and further, show how individual disciplinary perspectives address questions about related topics. Far from engaging in random interaction, children are always seeking to build knowledge through their play and questions. A skilled play-based educator can use children's natural curiosity to launch deeper investigations into topics of interest. For example, imagine a classroom of preschoolers who have noticed the birds that live along the perimeter of the school playground. Their innocent questions about bird sounds, homes, and social communities might inspire their teachers to support a deeper classroom investigation.

What do we notice and wonder about these birds? What questions do we have? How might different experts—such as mathematicians, zoologists, or musicians—approach the task of exploring our questions? What unique tools or evidence might they employ in their pursuit of knowledge? How might their learnings connect to tell a cohesive story about the birds around our school? Approaching learning in this play-based, curiosity-forward way allows children to build cognitive, social, and emotional skills; and, evidence consistently shows that play-based learning leads to better academic outcomes in the long run (e.g., Hirsh-Pasek et al., 2009).

THE "A" OF STEAM: WHY IT MATTERS

Early childhood STEM education and research has historically focused on building foundational numeracy skills and an understanding of the natural sciences for young children (Bers, 2008; Bers et al., 2013; Moomaw & Davis, 2010). The concept of promoting creativity and expression through technology and the sciences is articulated in the acronym called "STEAM" (science, technology, engineering, *arts*, mathematics) that we use throughout this book. In practice, the "A" of STEAM can represent the whole spectrum of the liberal arts, including language arts, social studies, music, culture, history, and more.

Within an early childhood context, integrated STEAM education means finding ways for children to explore these subjects in an integrated way through hands-on projects, books, discussions, experiments, art explorations, collaboration, games, and play. The result is well-informed learners who are able to apply problem-solving skills to a wide range of interdisciplinary subjects. For example, Maguth (2012) proposed that social studies content should be integrated into a STEM-focused curriculum in order to promote the development of well-rounded citizens prepared for voting on ethical and social issues related to STEM. Other research by Pugh and Girod (2007) advocates for an integrated approach to science education that combines scientific inquiry with artistic experience. They provide evidence that such an interdisciplinary approach enhances students' engagement and deepens their understanding by connecting scientific concepts to real-world experiences.

Other research has also demonstrated powerful interdisciplinary connections between children's STEM skills and other important areas like language and literacy. For example, a randomized study of the Building Blocks math curriculum showed that the curriculum led to higher scores on measures of early language and literacy, such as the ability to recognize letters and gain oral language skills like expressing one's knowledge and understanding spoken words (Sarama et al., 2012). Other research has shown the connection between language and later math skills. For example, one study showed that exposure to more spatial language during block play in infancy and early childhood increases children's spatial abilities when they are older (Pruden et al., 2011).

When we look at STEAM throughout history, it is surprising that STEM education has not always integrated the arts. Historically, there have been countless brilliant innovators, such as Leonardo da Vinci and Frank Lloyd Wright, who have seamlessly woven together the fields of art and science in their work (Sullivan et al., 2017). Many modern innovations have also resulted from an integration of the arts with STEM. For example, the computer chips that run almost all of our digital devices are made using a combination of three classic artistic inventions: etching, silk screen printing, and photolithography (Root-Bernstein, 2011). It is even estimated that Nobel laureates in the sciences are 17 times likelier than the average scientist to be a painter, 12 times as likely to be a poet, and 4 times as likely to be a musician (Pomeroy, 2012). This is probably because the arts, like science, technology, engineering, and mathematics, are rooted in a similar mindset of curiosity and creativity.

In Part II of this book, we will build on the importance of integrated STEAM learning and explore pedagogies and teaching approaches to put STEAM into practice in your own playful learning setting. Taking this interdisciplinary approach to fostering playful STEAM learning, we will discuss integrating books, music, dramatic play, and more to explore domains like science, math, coding, and engineering. The end goal will be well-rounded and engaged youth who are able to think critically about a variety of real-world issues. The integration of the arts will also help to reach and support confidence, competence, and a positive STEAM identity with students who have not been interested, supported in, or encouraged to pursue the sciences.

THE PLAYFUL STEAM LEARNING FRAMEWORK

Whether you choose to explore STEAM through tangible toys and technologies, hands-on sensory experiments, or just outside in nature, it is important to take a playful approach to teaching and learning with young students. Not only does this engage children in the self-rewarding cycle of joyful STEAM engagement, but it also activates the ideal state of mind to foster long-term, self-directed learning while also supporting a positive STEAM identity development. The Playful STEAM Learning Framework provides parents, caregivers, and educators with guidelines on how best to support young children's learning through STEAM play in early childhood—without the use of screen time.

The most important piece of the framework goes back to what we have been discussing all throughout this chapter: play! Play is at the heart of how young children learn, socialize, and make authentic discoveries. Play supports children's development of intellectual curiosity that builds the foundation for their learning across all domains. Therefore, the PSLF is rooted in a combination of child-led and adult-scaffolded play experiences. The framework identifies three overarching play approaches, specific strategies educators can implement, as well as evaluation approaches that can be implemented in both formal and informal learning settings.

While other frameworks and conceptual models for STEAM learning exist (e.g., Quigley et al., 2017; Yakman, 2010, 2011), the PSLF is unique in its focus on early childhood, play, and centering the child's play experiences. The approaches presented in the framework are rooted in Papert's constructionist educational framework and previous work that explores how children learn through hands-on activities (Papert, 1980, 2000). Constructionism explains that children learn deeply when engaged in building digital projects that are meaningful for them, when participating in a community of learners, and when reflecting on the process of digital creation (including in off-screen technology contexts) (Papert, 1980, 2000). This framework is rooted in Piaget's constructivism, which emphasizes "learning by doing" and claims that children build knowledge through experience (Ackermann, 2001; Mascolo & Fischer, 2005). These two approaches, when applied to playful STEAM learning, mean that learners construct knowledge by solving real-world problems using hands-on materials and playful explorations in both physical and digital contexts.

We further root our Playful STEAM Learning Framework in the Positive Technological Development (PTD) framework developed by Dr. Marina Umaschi Bers (Bers, 2020), but we expand to consider technology-free learning settings. The PTD framework guides the development, implementation, and evaluation of educational programs that use new technologies to promote learning as an aspect of positive youth development through teaching "6 Cs" when using technology: content creation, creativity, communication, collaboration, community building, and choices of conduct. We build on Bers's 6 Cs and suggest that these positive behaviors can also be fostered during technology-free STEAM learning and play.

The Playful STEAM Learning Framework highlights three broad approaches to play that are particularly relevant to STEAM learning: curiosity-based, child-led, and authentic. All kinds of play (sensory, parallel, etc.) can fall into our broadly defined play approaches (see Table 2.1). We chose these play approaches to help you remember the "educational goal" of your play facilitation. These approaches are developmentally appropriate for the young age we are focused on and uniquely supportive of STEAM identity building:

- **Curiosity-based play** supports children's questions and helps develop their intellectual curiosity through play.
- **Child-led play** lets children take the lead in their playful learning experiences.
- **Authentic play** supports children engaging in learning that is personally and culturally meaningful to them.

Table 2.1. Strategies and Evaluation to Support the Core Three Play Approaches of the Playful STEAM Learning Framework

Play Approach	Strategies	Evaluation
Curiosity-Based	Offer opportunities for experimentation based on children's questions. Celebrate children's questions with a running "Question Wall" to display questions that come up throughout the day. Foster a "curiosity cycle" where one discovery leads to new child-led questions to explore.	Use observation to tell the story of the play: What questions did children have that sparked the play? What (if any) problem were children solving? What project was developed through their play? *Ex: Photo journal with child quotes of a child's building projects with LEGO sparked by a child's curiosity and questions about different styles of architecture*
Child-Led	Let children lead explorations without intervening. Pause, observe, and assume the role of a co-learner or facilitator, rather than director or leader of the learning. Encourage children to learn by doing (not only by watching/following).	Represent child-made work without editing or improving it. *Ex: Artifacts collected over the course of school year showing how the child's ideas about color mixing evolved*
Authentic	Support authentic and immersive play through a mix of guided and free play opportunities. Support youth voice and choice by offering different ways for children to guide their own playful learning experience to make it personally and/or culturally meaningful to them. Offer authentic opportunities for children to share their learning and give/receive recognition from peers and other adults. Encourage children to share their experience and feelings about the project (not just their learning).	Provide structures for children to present their own work. *Ex: Child-led showcase of a robot they designed and built for their family visit day at summer camp*

The three play approaches highlighted in Table 2.1, which can be relevant to both STEAM and non-STEAM domains, are vehicles to support the four pillars of the Playful STEAM Learning Framework: (1) Persevering through hard fun, (2) Listening to children's ideas, (3) Actively supporting inclusion, and (4) Saying Yes to open-ended sensory play. Using the acronym **PLAY** to remember these four pillars also serves as a reminder that at the heart of all of the most powerful early learning experiences are smiling, laughter, and playing.

The four PLAY pillars are the building blocks of rewarding, motivating, and engaging STEAM learning in early childhood and beyond. They can be used to guide educator and caregiver practice throughout development and are especially useful to build from toddler to elementary, or novice to advanced, STEAM play. The goal of these pillars is to help children learn to independently persevere through the "hard fun" of the sciences and engineering in order to find joy in making discoveries, and to foster a lifelong learning approach to education.

Throughout this book, and particularly in Chapters 5–7, which focus on pedagogy, we will return to the Playful STEAM Learning Framework and the four building blocks or pillars of PLAY (see Table 2.2). Before that, it is important to briefly break down what is meant by each pillar in a bit more detail:

- **Persevering through hard fun:** What do we mean when we say "hard fun"? The term was coined by a programming pioneer named Alan Kay and was used to describe any activity that is both challenging and enjoyable. Hard fun activities help children (or adults!) learn how to manage frustration and gain confidence. Within education, hard fun activities allow students to experiment, make mistakes, and master new skills. For example, while learning to play music by turning on the radio might be "easy fun," learning to play music on the piano might be "hard fun." You may not "get it" right away, but through learning, practice, and perseverance, there is a big payoff that can be quite enjoyable in a different way. The same is true of many other STEAM activities, such as coding and engineering. For example, while it might be easy fun to play with a preprogrammed robot toy, it would be hard fun to learn how to build and code your own interactive robot. (Yes, this is really something young children can do beginning in preschool!). The activities and approaches in this book will focus on ways to keep the playful, fun spirit in STEAM activities, even when they do not necessarily come easily to children or when they spark frustration because of a steep learning curve.
- **Listening to children's ideas:** Throughout this book, we will continually return to the idea of helping children learn through personally meaningful play experiences. In order to hone in on

Table 2.2. The Playful STEAM Learning Framework in Practice: The Educator's Role

	Pillars of the Playful STEAM Learning Framework			
	P—Persevering through hard fun	**L—Listening to children's ideas**	**A—Actively supporting inclusion**	**Y—Saying Yes to open-ended sensory play**
Curiosity-Based Play	Educators support children through frustration so they can make a discovery about something they are curious about.	Educators create a culture of valuing curiosity by tracking children's questions and providing opportunities to answer questions and test ideas through play and experimentation.	Educators ensure all children have a voice in terms of the projects and play experiences that are facilitated.	Educators provide sensory materials for exploration that children are curious about, even if there may not be a specific "learning goal" from the start.
Child-Led Play	Educators foster a culture of learning from mistakes that allows children to take the lead even in challenging explorations.	Educators regularly take children's suggestions for STEAM projects, centers, and explorations.	Educators make STEM play more accessible and interesting to a wider range of children by incorporating the arts, music, literature, and other domains children are passionate about (i.e., a STEAM approach).	Educators provide children with choices for messy and hands-on STEAM exploration.
Authentic Play	Educators provide authentic ways for students to share knowledge and receive recognition after persevering through challenging STEAM play.	Educators provide opportunities for Project-Based Learning (PBL) to explore authentic projects that children are invested in.	Educators meet children's individual needs by providing different ways to engage with STEAM play.	Educators provide a mix of materials that are personally and culturally relevant to children.

what experiences will be personally meaningful for different young children, it is important to truly listen to their ideas. Let's return to the idea of free play introduced earlier in this chapter. Free play is child-directed and relies on minimal adult involvement. In free play, children may take the lead in planning their play and carrying out their plan, making adjustments along the way. This process is important because it helps support the development of self-regulation, internal language (self-talk), and working memory (Lockhart, 2010). Throughout this book, we will explore how we can encourage young children to take the lead in their playful learning by positioning adults as guides, facilitators, co-learners, or even playmates. We will explore strategies for adults to foster a combination of free play and guided play that still embodies a child-centered approach, placing children as the directors of their own learning. When it comes to curriculum development, the PSLF advocates for a flexible, emergent pedagogical approach that gives children a strong voice in their own learning.

- **Actively supporting inclusion:** Ensuring that the approaches, opportunities, and pathways to succeed in STEAM are inclusive, welcoming, and encouraging of all learners regardless of gender identity, race, culture, or socioeconomic status is at the heart of the mission of this book. There are now many digital tools, such as robotics kits and digital games, available for young children to explore STEAM. But many of these new tools, despite their benefits, are inaccessible based on the cost, technical support, and professional development needed to implement them properly (Sullivan & Strawhacker, 2021). This growing digital divide is one of the main reasons behind the screen-free and unplugged approaches presented in this book. Furthermore, many of the existing high-tech resources, initiatives, and curricula related to engineering and computer science are not welcoming or inclusive of girls and other groups persistently underrepresented in technical STEM fields (Sullivan, 2019). The Playful STEAM Learning Framework and the associated strategies presented within this book will strive for inclusivity by providing free and low-cost options to explore computing, engineering, and the sciences. They will encourage collaborative, artistic, and creative sides to fields typically portrayed as serious and solitary. Most of all, they will provide curricular approaches that are easily adapted and modified to reach young children in a variety of settings and with a diversity of abilities and interests, in order to create a more welcoming introduction to the world of STEAM.
- **Saying Yes to open-ended sensory play:** In Chapter 1, we talked about sand and water tables. We talked about slime. We talked about

jumping in puddles, playing in mud, and swinging on swings. We talked about messy, dirty, sensory explorations that bring young children joy. These experiences are not necessarily focused on creating a product or reaching a specific outcome. Instead, they are processes of child-led sensory explorations that are often, well, messy. According to Duffy (2007), "messy play" involves (1) children using their senses in the process of exploration, especially the sense of touch; (2) offering children plenty of opportunity to mold and manipulate materials; and, (3) much like sensory play examples described earlier in Chapter 1, it does not necessarily have a focus on making or producing something specific. We used these examples to help remind adults that playing with young children can be (and often is, whether we plan it or not) messy business. After all, there is no better way to learn about the world than by touching it, experiencing it, or even breaking it and shaping it. Messy, sensory play is part of children's need to closely investigate different substances, and is required for creative experiments that involve learning through chaos (Szekely, 2015). In short, sensory play is one of the most important types of play for young children to engage in for learning. Throughout this book, we will place an emphasis on sensory early childhood experiences that promote meaningful STEAM engagement and development.

CONCLUDING THOUGHTS

It may look like simple fun, or even wasted time, but play is essential to growing, developing, and learning. The neurological state of mind that play induces allows our brains to relax, recharge, and form new connections between existing concepts and ideas. This connection is critical to learning in all domains and builds the foundation for more complex connections to grow into fully formed theories and knowledge about the world. A regular play practice in early childhood allows children to progress through developmental play milestones, growing more collaborative, organized, and intentional in their play, and in their thinking. Learning in the technical fields of computer science, engineering, and computational thinking is no exception. When playing with mechanical tools, construction processes, or computational logic, children are engaged in the same kind of free-form idea exploration that professional scientists and engineers engage in when problem-solving and experimenting. Play sets the stage for perseverance, curiosity, and skills development long into adulthood, preparing today's toddlers to become tomorrow's STEAM leaders. In the next chapter, we will explore how we can apply the playful STEAM learning framework to teaching and learning how to code—all without the use of any computers!

CHAPTER 3

Computational Thinking Without Computers

In every other chapter of this book, we talk broadly about playful ways to support educational STEAM–integrated STEM and the arts. But this book presents a big claim, which is that it is possible to successfully teach foundational STEAM content to 2–8-year-olds without any kind of screen-based tools. In most STEAM disciplines, this is actually a self-evident idea, since variations of science, math, engineering, and the arts were being taught in early education long before personal computing devices became commonplace. *Technology*, however, might seem like one domain that naturally requires screens to teach disciplinary principles in a meaningful way. In order to support the claim that STEAM play can be rich and educational without screens of any kind, this chapter unpacks specific learning goals and opportunities available to young children in the realm of technology and presents arguments for why we maintain that these learning goals are screen-agnostic and achievable in traditional early learning settings.

WHAT IS COMPUTATIONAL THINKING?

Travel back in time for a moment to the year 2015. The computer science education movement was gaining a lot of public interest, and leaders in the field like Alan Kay (called the "father of personal computers") were posing questions about how to teach computer coding as a literacy and how to democratize computer science from a young age so children could learn to build their own computerized tools and ideas. Code.org, an education nonprofit, had been founded just 2 years earlier with the mission of bringing computer science (CS) education into schools across the country. As part of that mission, Code.org coordinated a K-12 computer science thought leaders convening in November 2015, to gather researchers, educators, and policymakers to shape the curricular and pedagogical vision for CS education in the United States. Code.org's chief academic officer, Pat Yongpradit, invited CS education expert professor Marina Bers to send an expert to speak from the early childhood education perspective. She sent her then-doctoral student Amanda Strawhacker (one of the authors of this book) to convene and represent the current research and best practices related to computer science in early childhood education.

Leaving the airport in a taxi on the way to the convention, Pat asked Amanda a question. As it turns out, this question would foreshadow a career-defining perspective for Amanda in the years to come. He asked, "Don't you agree that kids need an actual computer to learn about computer science?" Amanda's immediate and confident reply surprised him: "No." He asked more and more questions, like how children could possibly learn about a thing without seeing or touching it? Amanda admitted that that would be ridiculous, especially for 4-to-7-year-olds. But after some reflection she tried to explain her reasoning: "We don't care if children learn 'computers.' We want them to learn how to think."

Computational thinking is cited as a major goal behind computer and technology-based interventions, and it represents a constellation of skills including mathematical abilities; reasoning skills such as conditional reasoning, analogical reasoning, and temporal reasoning; as well as procedural thinking and memory capacity (Denning & Tedre, 2019a; 2019b; Lodi & Martini, 2021; Wing, 2006). Sometimes policymakers and researchers summarize these skills as "thinking like a computer" (e.g., Denning & Tedre, 2019b). Although this is a helpful definition, it is not exactly accurate. In reality, most educators don't necessarily want children to think like a computer. "Thinking" is something that a computer does in a very scripted, specific, and linear way. Computers rarely make true mistakes, but they often leave users frustrated or even convinced that the computer is working against them. This is because they aren't clever enough to fix silly typos in their own code, explain what to do if you receive an error message, or recognize what a human user likely wanted but didn't know how to ask for. It can be a bit like speaking to a robot on an automated phone line that doesn't have your specific question programmed into the recording. Probably most educators and parents would agree that we actually hope children will learn how to think flexibly, creatively, and freely. So why explore computers at all?

A computer, at its core, is a simplistic and rather poor imitation of a human brain (e.g., Huang, 2017). Even the most cutting-edge computers powered by artificial intelligence are still clunky when it comes to human-like reasoning and abstraction abilities (Panagiotopoulos, 2024). However, because of their simplicity in faithfully following an algorithm, computers can be useful tools for helping children—even very young ones—play with notions of logic, cause and effect, and sequencing. These concepts describe how computers function, and computers can make logic feel hands-on and visible to children. But logic and sequencing are also foundational to ancient human systems of numeracy, literacy, and even society. Humans never could have invented computers in the first place without these critical structures of algorithmic, procedural, and mathematical reasoning. They support metacognition, or "thinking about thinking," which CS education researchers like Seymour Papert argue is the foundation of reflective learning (Papert & Harel, 1991). More importantly, they are the skills we hope children engage with when we introduce learning interventions with computers.

If we agree that computational thinking does not require a computer, how can we invite young children to build skills of sequencing, logic, and metacognition without screens? In this chapter, we draw clear divides between learning opportunities available with screen-based devices and screen-free/unplugged STEAM experiences. We ask the question, "How can (and why) should children learn foundational computing concepts without computers?"

CODING, COMPUTER SCIENCE (CS), AND COMPUTATIONAL THINKING (CT)

Computer education terms are sometimes used interchangeably, but there are some important differences (see Table 3.1). Before we think about how to teach these concepts, let's begin with some helpful definitions. Under each definition, we've included simple phrases that you can use to explain these ideas to young children.

As you read through the definitions, you might notice that it may not be feasible to explore all of these concepts in an off-screen setting. For example, children probably *do* need access to computers to understand computer science lessons about how to identify whether a machine is alive, how to type on a keyboard, how to move a mouse, and how to use a screen interface. A coding lesson about how to write and test code in a specific coding language necessarily requires a robot or computer that can understand the coding language. Some broader concepts are more accessible with technologies, as well. For example, when teaching about the distinction between human and machine languages, it makes sense to allow children to write code and observe how a machine interprets it, compared to how we humans communicate with each other.

In other areas, devices are not as necessary. We do not need computers to teach about coding logic and computational thinking (CT). Since CT encompasses a broad array of thought patterns, it is helpful to break it down further into manageable learning goals. The United Kingdom began adopting a nationwide curricular initiative to introduce computer science in K–12 settings over a decade ago in 2014 (Fowler & Vegas, 2021). In addition to teacher training and curriculum and device access, leaders found that defining critical CT learning outcomes was key to the success of this wide-reaching program (Fowler & Vegas, 2021). According to the BBC, UK schools now emphasize four cornerstones of computational thinking: decomposition, pattern recognition, abstraction, and algorithms (BBC, 2024):

Table 3.1. Definitions of Common Concepts in Computer Education

Computational Concept	Definition	Child-Friendly Definition
Code	The written instructions that make up software, which gives directions that control computer hardware (machinery). Code is written in special nonhuman languages that communicate information so a computer can interpret it.	Special instructions written to tell computers what to do. It's like a secret language that computers understand.
Coding	Writing, testing, and editing the written code of any software system, to create or refine how it controls the computer.	Writing and fixing the special instructions (code) to make computers do things, like playing games or showing pictures.
Computer Science (CS)	The study of computers, including the function and use of hardware and software.	Learning about how computers work and how we can use them to do things.
Computational Thinking (CT)	Thinking in a logical and systematic way, using sequenced algorithms much like a computer would. May include mathematical, procedural, algorithmic, chronological, and logical thinking strategies.	Thinking step-by-step and very carefully, just like a computer, to solve problems.

- *Decomposition*: Invites students to break down complex problems into smaller, simpler problems.
- *Pattern Recognition*: Guides students to make connections between similar problems and experiences.
- *Abstraction*: Encourages students to identify important information while ignoring unrelated or irrelevant details.
- *Algorithms*: Involves designing simple steps to solve problems.

As you read through the definitions of these cornerstones of CT, challenge yourself to consider ways that all of these goals can be taught effectively through unplugged activities. Perhaps you already focus on decomposition in math class, when students need to break large numbers into friendly landmark amounts to solve an equation. Pattern recognition is a useful literacy and language arts practice when children need to identify patterns in word phonemes (e.g., blended letter sounds, short and long vowel sounds, common word endings) that help them make predictions about how to pronounce and use new words. Students might be exposed to abstraction during a social studies unit on maps as representations of neighborhoods, cities, and countries. In science class, they may already use algorithms to build experiments and test hypotheses in a step-by-step way, following the scientific method.

Once again, we see that the foundations of computational thinking need not be restricted to the realm of computer class, but can be fostered throughout the day in countless hands-on, authentic, and developmentally appropriate contexts. The next section outlines what empirical research has to say on the success of unplugged education interventions to support CT learning.

EVIDENCE FOR UNPLUGGED CT LEARNING

Research has shown that young children can effectively develop computational thinking skills without the need for computers, using unplugged activities in early childhood and elementary school settings. For instance, Brackmann et al. (2017) explored the development of CT skills through hands-on workshops where children engaged in activities designed to teach concepts of decomposition, pattern recognition, abstraction, and algorithm design. Students explored activities such as writing down the steps required to plant a tree; making an algorithm to describe how to sing a song; drawing and rotating geometric Tetris shapes; and using board game–inspired maps to plan efficient routes. Researchers found significant improvements in the children's logical and systematic thinking abilities, demonstrating that CT skills can be nurtured without the use of computers.

Similarly, studies of unplugged tasks in formal education settings have yielded promising results. Messer et al. (2018) investigated the impact of educational programming interventions on various cognitive skills, including algorithmic thinking (i.e., problem-solving through creating a series of systematic, logical steps), in children. Forty-one 5-to-6-year olds from a UK school were randomly allocated to one of three groups: programming tasks using iPad technology, programming tasks using paper and pencils, and a comparison condition involving pencil-and-paper mathematical addition and subtraction tasks. Results revealed that all three groups increased their mathematical abilities and spatial awareness. Importantly, there were no significant differences between any of the groups, even when comparing algorithmic programming task performance of the iPad group and the paper-and-pencil group. These results support the idea that unplugged interventions can have broad cognitive benefits, reinforcing the value of CT education without screens. In a separate study on computational thinking in older students, Rodriguez et al. (2016) evaluated the effectiveness of CS Unplugged activities in middle school classroom environments. CS

Unplugged is a collection of free teaching materials created by computer science experts (and funded by technology companies like Google and Microsoft) that teaches computer science through games, puzzles, and traditional hands-on manipulatives (csunplugged.org). This study specifically sought to evaluate student learning by assessing performance on lesson tasks. Their findings provided empirical evidence that unplugged activities not only engage students but also lead to measurable improvements in CT skills. This supports the use of unplugged activities in classrooms as a valid and effective method for teaching CT, making it a practical approach for educators.

In the context of young students, experiences that are situated in real-life contexts are most impactful for long-term learning. Relkin and Strawhacker (2021) emphasize the importance of recognizing CT skills in everyday life and describe how many daily tasks, such as following a recipe or organizing a play area, inherently involve CT principles. Their research highlights how these everyday activities can naturally help children see the relevance of CT skills and develop fluency with them more quickly.

Collectively, these studies suggest that unplugged CT interventions are both successful and developmentally appropriate for early childhood and elementary schooling. These interventions make CT education accessible to young children while promoting a broad range of cognitive skills without relying on screens. This approach aligns with the natural learning processes of young children, integrating CT principles into their everyday experiences and activities.

PRACTICAL APPROACHES TO UNPLUGGED COMPUTATIONAL THINKING

Throughout this book, we present strategies and practices to integrate STEAM into your screen-free early childhood and elementary education setting. If you want to focus specifically on computational thinking in your practice, several evidence-based suggestions can get you started.

There are a variety of ways for students to practice computational thinking skills long before they ever try computer programming. One of the easiest ways to help students get started is to find the ways your classroom already practices computational thinking, so you can name it and make those connections very visible to students. By recognizing and labeling these practices, educators can help students see the connections between computational thinking and other subjects like science, math, and language arts. For example, educators are already exploring the CT skill of sequencing whenever they talk about order of events (e.g., when discussing the daily schedule or during math practice), and they are exploring the CT skill of decomposition when discussing how students can break down a big task into smaller, more manageable parts (e.g., when working on a large project, such as multiphase art project).

Another reliable way to build computational thinking into your educational practice is to integrate CT into other subjects to make it concrete and relevant for students. In all domains, research consistently confirms that children respond to hands-on, playful activities (Zosh et al., 2022). Choose tasks that emphasize logic and systematic problem-solving to foster CT. Sequencing activities, for instance, encourage children to create step-by-step instructions for everyday tasks, such as brushing their teeth or planting a seed. This helps them understand the importance of order and cause and effect, which are foundational to algorithmic thinking. Additionally, pattern recognition games, such as matching games or puzzles, require them to identify patterns and make connections between different elements. This can be as simple as sorting objects by color, shape, or size, which builds their ability to recognize and utilize patterns in more complex contexts.

Decomposition exercises are effective strategies. By breaking down larger projects into smaller, manageable parts, children can learn how to approach complex tasks incrementally. For example, building a simple model or completing a multistep art project can teach them how to tackle problems by breaking them into smaller, more manageable tasks. This approach not only makes challenging projects more accessible but also builds confidence and problem-solving skills.

Algorithm design is another crucial component of computational thinking that can be taught without computers. Children can create simple algorithms for tasks they perform regularly, such as making a sandwich or getting ready for school. This activity fosters their ability to think systematically and logically, reinforcing the step-by-step nature of algorithms that they will later encounter in computer science.

Role-playing and storytelling can also be powerful tools for teaching computational thinking. Through role-playing games and storytelling, children can illustrate concepts of abstraction and algorithmic thinking by acting out scenarios that require them to follow specific rules or steps to achieve a goal. For example, a role-playing game where they pretend to be chefs following a recipe can help them understand the importance of sequence and accuracy in completing a task. Picture books and songs are excellent tools for the youngest learners to understand order and sequence, and how these elements contribute to the consistency and predictability of a story.

Finally, seek out free resources from websites such as CSUnplugged.org, Code.org, and Code.org's CS Fundamentals Unplugged. In addition to being vetted by hundreds of students and classrooms, these resources are often designed for learners as young as 4 years old.

By integrating these activities into early childhood education, we can foster computational thinking skills without relying on screens. These foundational skills not only prepare children for future learning in computer science but also enhance their overall cognitive development, problem-solving abilities, and creative thinking. Moreover, these activities align with the natural learning processes of young children, making CT principles part of their everyday experiences and activities.

CONCLUDING THOUGHTS

While computers are valuable tools for teaching certain aspects of computer science, they are not necessary for developing the fundamental skills associated with computational thinking. Through carefully designed unplugged activities, educators can help young children build a strong foundation in logical reasoning, problem-solving, and systematic thinking that will serve them well in all areas of learning and life. By focusing on hands-on, playful approaches to teaching CT, educators can ensure that all children, regardless of their access to technology, can develop these critical skills. This approach not only makes computational thinking more accessible but also supports a more holistic and inclusive education that values creativity, problem-solving, and critical thinking. Furthermore, incorporating CT through integrated STEAM learning can facilitate young children's connection to this important learning domain in concrete and lasting ways. The remainder of this book explores this approach and describes strategies to highlight the inextricable link between STEAM learning and playful, real-life experiences.

CHAPTER 4

Access, Equity, and Inclusion in STEAM

Despite widespread support of STEM and STEAM education movements, issues of equity and access have remained a continuing challenge in STEM careers and educational settings. This is particularly true in areas of technology and engineering, which lack diversity in both higher education and professional settings. Women, particularly women of color, have been historically excluded from many STEM fields. Women constitute approximately half of the workforce in the U.S. but only 35% of the STEM workforce (National Girls Collaborative Project, 2024). According to the National Girls Collaborative Project's (NGCP) most recent *State of Girls and Women in STEM* publication, women currently earn only 24% of bachelor's degrees in engineering and only 21% of bachelor's degrees in computer science (NGCP, 2024). Black, Hispanic, and Indigenous women represent less than 10% of the STEM workforce and women only 16% of engineers and 26% of computer scientists (NGCP, 2024).

These numbers are staggering, especially considering how rapidly technology and engineering fields are growing in the United States. Not only are women, particularly women of color, missing out on potentially rewarding and lucrative careers in these fast-growing scientific and engineering fields, but the lack of proper representation in these fields also leads to other ethical issues. When women are excluded from the fields that drive the design and creation of technical innovations that we all rely on, the result is rampant biases in product design such as smartphones that don't fit women's hands as well as men's hands (Dinamani & Shibley, 2023) and cars and crash test dummies designed and modeled after men, leaving women more likely to be injured in an automotive accident (Perez, 2019).

Most of us would agree that we need diverse voices in these scientific and engineering industries. Still, you might be wondering what this has to do with a book focused on early childhood education. Addressing issues of equity in STEM careers begins long before students are entering college or the workforce. It is critical to provide every student, beginning in early childhood, with high-quality STEM and STEAM opportunities, regardless of race, ethnicity, geography, income level, and disability status in order to set them up for success in these fields later in life. And in fact, as we will explore, research has demonstrated that early childhood is a pivotal time to begin sparking curiosity and interest in STEM and STEAM, especially for youth who have been historically excluded from these fields. Throughout this chapter, we will explore what it means to support equitable early STEAM experiences and the important role that early childhood educators play.

DEFINING EQUITY

Let's take a step back and define *equity* before we go any further. Equity considers the specific needs or circumstances of a person or group and provides the types of resources needed to be successful. It may not mean everyone gets the same thing. Instead, it means everyone gets what they require to meet their needs, thrive, and be successful in a given activity or environment. For example, for all students in a 2nd-grade classroom to be successful engaging with a book about oceans, it may not be enough to give each child the same book. Some students may need to read the book in Spanish, some may need to read it in English, some may need to receive an audio version of the book, and others may need a Braille version. Considering these individual needs of your students is at the heart of creating an equitable learning environment.

We conceptualize equity as a *process*, something to constantly be working toward. It is a way of approaching education with the lens of supporting all students through engaging and rigorous STEAM education that they can connect with in a meaningful way, grappling with and challenging systemic racism, power, and oppression; and using STEM to empower themselves and their communities (Madkins et al., 2020).

While equity goes far beyond simply addressing issues of access, that is often the first piece of the puzzle. In computer science education, for example, inequities rooted in access are pervasive. This includes students' access to necessary technology, elementary school learning opportunities, advanced course offerings in later schooling years, and access to qualified teachers who utilize effective teaching strategies (Brannon & Novak, 2019; Fancsali, 2022; Howard & Havard, 2019; Howard & Howard, 2020; Madkins et al., 2019; Margolis & Goode, 2016). Using the unplugged approaches presented in the Playful STEAM Framework throughout this book is one strategy for overcoming the impacts of persistent disparities in the area of computer science that are rooted in technology access.

To improve the overall quality of STEAM programs, we must address these pervasive issues of access beginning in early childhood. This means ensuring that all youth have access to high-quality STEAM opportunities and feel welcome in STEM and STEAM. The Access to STEM Framework developed by the National Girls Collaborative Project for the STEM Next Opportunity Fund (NGCP, 2022) explains the following strategies and tactics for increasing access and creating equitable spaces for all learners in the sciences. These strategies address barriers to participation and build on the experiences within the community:

- **Community engagement:** Create plans for internal and external communication and outreach; build cross-sector partnerships to cultivate a STEM learning ecosystem; offer community and family engagement opportunities.
- **Data-informed decision-making:** Identify ways to collect youth and program-level data to improve program quality; collect feedback from youth and families; conduct evaluation to assess broader community needs.
- **Program design (quality and intentionality):** Involve stakeholders who represent the community and offer diverse perspectives in program design; form an advisory board with key stakeholders to provide ongoing guidance and feedback; be intentional in program design to engage and effectively serve all youth.
- **Program operations:** Ensure all youth have access to programming (location, schedule, transportation, technology); ensure all youth feel welcome (broad outreach to diverse populations, marketing designed to engage all youth, welcoming environment); recruit and retain staff who are representative of the community.

The strategies and tactics outlined in the framework provide educators, program directors, and other invested parties with approaches for setting up and facilitating equitable STEAM programs and experiences.

STEREOTYPES AND EARLY CHILDHOOD

Sometimes improving access to classes, curriculum, and tech tools isn't enough to improve engagement for children from groups that have been historically excluded from technology and the sciences. This is because many barriers to entry in these fields are rooted in larger systems of inequality. Decades of pervasive exposure to stereotypes about who "can" and "should" pursue the sciences, for example, have a profound impact on all of us—whether we believe these stereotypes to be true or not.

A stereotype is a widely held but fixed and oversimplified image or idea about a specific group. Stereotypes may relate to gender, sex, race, ethnicity, age, professions, hobbies, and more. Whether you believe a stereotype to be true or not, it can still have a profound impact on your performance and identification with STEM. Research has shown that stereotypes contribute to achievement and opportunity gaps among racial, ethnic, gender, and cultural groups, and these stereotypes begin to form earlier than you may think. Research has shown that stereotypes about girls' interest in computer science and engineering, for example, are formed as early as age 6 and are evident across multiple ages from childhood through adolescence (Master et al., 2021).

Early childhood is a critical time for piquing the interest of girls and other historically excluded groups in STEAM (Sullivan, 2019). In areas like computer science, where the gender disparity is particularly apparent, early exposure may be a key component to overcoming long-term barriers. Research has demonstrated that exposure to computer programming can promote young children's motivation to engage with computer science materials, especially for girls (Master et al., 2017). Early, positive exposure to STEM fields like computer science can help counter the impact of negative societal stereotypes about girls and computer science (Code.org et al., 2024; Master et al., 2023; Sullivan, 2021). A focus on STEAM programming in the foundational early childhood and early elementary years means that these experiences will also come at a critical time in young children's learning and development, a time when positive associations are easier to form (Wang & Degol, 2017).

STEM/STEAM IDENTITY

Stereotypes are just one of the barriers that prevent girls, particularly girls of color, from identifying with science, technology, engineering, and mathematics. STEM identity development is conceptualized by researchers as both a reflection of how one perceives and positions oneself within STEM, and how one is perceived and recognized by meaningful others (Carlone & Johnson, 2007). In short, STEM identity refers to the extent to which individuals identify and view themselves as members of a STEM field (Hachey, 2020; Kim et al., 2018).

Carlone and Johnson (2007) provide a model for science identity that includes competence, performance, and recognition. Using this model as a guide, we see a process for STEAM identity development that includes learning and becoming competent in STEAM concepts, performing these concepts or skills in an authentic way, and then receiving recognition from others (such as educators, peers, etc.). Through this process of performance and recognition, individuals begin to feel they belong in a particular STEAM field or in the enactment of integrated STEAM activities (Archer et al., 2017; Carlone et al., 2014; Hughes & Schellinger, 2023; Master et al., 2017).

The majority of research in the field of STEM identity is focused on adolescents and adults. In fact, much of identity-focused research in general is focused on the adolescent years. However, we know from the body of work on stereotypes that children form stereotypes, attitudes, and beliefs early about themselves (and others) as STEM/STEAM learners. Building on this, Hachey (2020) asserts that identity work *is* a task of early childhood, suggesting the need to focus on young children's engagement with STEM education as a means of nurturing their early STEM identity development. Young children gain school-related identities by acquiring language and behaviors needed to display the identity of a "successful student" (Hawkins, 2005). Applying this to STEAM contexts, supporting identification with STEM/STEAM in the early years can be done by fostering authentic STEAM-related practices and roles that contextualize early acquisition of STEAM content knowledge in authentic, meaningful, and positive ways (Hachey, 2020).

In order to develop a positive STEAM identity, learners must have opportunities to perform their competence in STEAM and be recognized for that competence by perceived experts (Calone & Johnson, 2007). A positive STEAM identity is one where students view themselves as capable, competent, and connected to the world of STEAM (Archer et al., 2022; Rahm & Moore, 2016). Building on the previous body of work on STEM and STEAM identity, the Playful STEAM Learning Framework, introduced in Chapter 2, hones in on the importance of authentic opportunities for giving and receiving meaningful feedback and recognition in order to foster children's identification with STEAM (see Table 4.1).

Table 4.1. Supporting a STEAM Identity With the Three Play Approaches of the Playful STEAM Learning Framework

	Supporting a STEAM Identity By . . .
Curiosity-Based Play	Providing opportunities for learners to gain **competence** in STEAM areas they are individually motivated and **curious** about.
Child-Led Play	Taking on the role of a **facilitator** or **co-learner** (rather than instructor) so that **children take the lead** in making discoveries and sparking their own "aha!" moments as they gain STEAM **competence** and **confidence** through their play.
Authentic Play	Providing opportunities for learners to **perform their skills** and knowledge through **real-world and authentic challenges** and projects, including long-term explorations. Providing opportunities for learners to **give and receive recognition** from peers, educators, and family or community through **meaningful** events and showcases that learners are invested in.

OVERCOMING BARRIERS: THE ROLE OF EDUCATORS

We know from research that there are many barriers for those historically excluded from the sciences, and we also know that early childhood is a pivotal time to start addressing these barriers. But how exactly, within formal and informal learning settings, can educators do this effectively? The truth is that addressing the ways in which systemic injustices manifest in educational practice remains a significant challenge in the study of teaching and learning (Artiles, 2011). This is because systemic injustices in the form of stereotypes and biases are often invisible to those involved with them.

In order to illustrate how educators might better support historically excluded students and decrease opportunity gaps, many scholars have introduced theoretical frameworks around the topic of educational equity. The pedagogical approaches grounded in these theoretical frameworks can be classified as equity pedagogies. These include culturally relevant pedagogy (CRP) (Ladson-Billings, 1995, 2012); culturally responsive teaching (CRT) (Gay, 2000); and culturally sustaining pedagogy (CSP) (Paris & Alim, 2014) (see Table 4.2).

Taken together, these approaches to education assert that all families are believed to have cultural capital, or knowledge, abilities, and networks

Table 4.2. Equity Pedagogies

Equity Pedagogy	Description
Culturally relevant pedagogy	CRP is a pedagogical framework devised by Dr. Gloria Ladson-Billings in the early 1990s. CRP rests on three fundamental pillars that work in tandem: academic achievement, cultural competence, and sociopolitical consciousness.
Culturally responsive teaching	CRT is a pedagogical approach devised by Geneva Gay in 2000 that focuses on situating academic knowledge and skills within the lived experiences and frames of reference of students. It means using students' customs, characteristics, experience, and perspectives as tools for better classroom teaching and learning.
Culturally sustaining pedagogy	CSP is a strengths-based instructional approach that centers and sustains the cultural and linguistic identities, experiences, and ways of knowing of diverse students and their families, caregivers, and communities.

that can, and should, be leveraged in classrooms. Each of these pedagogies, in different ways, positions educators to acknowledge, value, and leverage the wealth of knowledge found in communities that have been marginalized (Paris, 2012). At its heart, culturally responsive and sustaining education is about teaching the students in front of you. This requires that educators work to get to know their students and develop meaningful relationships with them while engaging in the students' communities.

We believe that interdisciplinary STEAM projects, beginning in the early years, provide an opportune way for educators to connect and build on the wealth of knowledge and traditions that their students have. Broughton and McClary (2020) outline nine ways that preschool educators can foster culturally responsive STEAM experiences in their early learning settings, including (1) inviting a diverse mix of community helpers to visit the classroom, (2) honor cultural knowledge, (3) connect with technology, (4) empower children with culturally responsive STEAM images, (5) express STEAM through cultural art, (6) connect math at home to the classroom, (7) incorporate cultural books, (8) launch a family STEAM invention project, and (9) continue to learn about children's cultures. We will draw on the equity pedagogies presented in this chapter and many of the approaches outlined by Broughton and McClary (2020) throughout Parts II and III of this book as we present curricular and practice-based suggestions, examples, and project prompts to support STEAM learning and play in an equitable fashion.

CONCLUDING THOUGHTS

We invite you, the reader, to consider the learners you serve—their backgrounds, interests, and cultures—as you read through the curriculum and approaches we present. We encourage you to think about adapting, remixing, and revising the suggestions we make to meet the individual needs of your learners and to celebrate and build on their culture and lived experiences. Moreover, we encourage you to take a moment to reflect on your own beliefs, practices, and biases. (We *all* have them.) Ask yourself: How do I talk about technology, math, and the sciences? Are there any stereotypes I am accidentally reinforcing through my own behavior and language? How do I address stereotypes about STEM that come up in children's play or during structured class time? How (or do) I build on my learners' cultural backgrounds? How (or do) I support all of my learners to engage with STEAM play in a way that is appropriate for them? As educators we often put a lot of focus on what children are saying and doing, but we rarely have time to devote to introspection. But when it comes to overcoming barriers and stereotypes, self-reflection is often the best place to start.

Part II

TEACHING STEAM IN EARLY CHILDHOOD CONTEXTS

CHAPTER 5

Exemplary Pedagogies and Practices for STEAM Integration

In early childhood education, much of the work of teaching happens before teachers even meet the children in a class, as teachers must craft environments and experiences ripe with learning opportunities, allowing children to take up what they are ready to investigate. Our Playful STEAM Learning Framework is designed to help teachers (and educators or caregivers of all kinds!) to think intentionally about planning environments and experiences, with an eye toward the *likely* (but beautifully unpredictable) questions. This chapter will introduce pedagogical philosophies related to educational environments (the Reggio Emilia approach, the Montessori method, the theory of loose parts, the affordance theory, and the Positive Technological Development Framework) that have informed our recommendations and provided the evidence for designing effective STEAM play opportunities. The purpose of this chapter is to situate our work within diverse pedagogical approaches that we believe contribute to rich, engaging learning environments and classroom communities that provide meaningful opportunities for young children to explore STEAM concepts.

LEARNING ENVIRONMENTS FOR STEAM EXPLORATION

Reggio Emilia Approach

We start with the Reggio Emilia approach, a fascinating educational theory named after the small town in Italy where it was created. During the post-World War II reconstruction efforts of this small village, which was completely decimated by the fighting, an enterprising teacher named Loris Malaguzzi developed an educational curriculum that involved the children directly in rebuilding and redesigning their own school and learning community. His approach elevated children to the status of equal and valued members of the town community, respected their wishes and ideas in designing a brand-new school, and emphasized collective action, democratic agency, and restorative justice in its very conception.

The Reggio Emilia classrooms of today manifest this philosophy in their aesthetically beautiful, "home"-inspired classrooms, designed to allow flexibility of action, thought, and activity for all children in the community. Unique aspects of Reggio Emilia–inspired environments include ateliers (literally, "workshops" or studios in French) designed by skilled atelierista educators: "environments promoting knowledge and creativity, suggesting questions and generating evocations; they are beauty that produces knowledge and vice-versa" (Reggio Children SRL, 2022). These environments feel very much like art exhibits, but are designed to be touched, played with, and experimented on by children (Gandini, 2005). Additionally, children often complete a portfolio of growth, a documented collection of their process through learning projects, during their time at a Reggio center.

As an educational philosophy, the Reggio Emilia approach holds two important learnings for us to emphasize. First, children are seen as individuals, with strong potential for learning and equally strong rights to agency, who express themselves through "a hundred languages," all symbolic and open to the endless potential of childhood. Second, the environment is viewed not just as important for children's learning but as a "third teacher," alongside adults (first teachers) and peers (second teachers) in the child's community. This means creating a flexible environment that is conducive to teachers and children creating and learning together.

Edwards (2011) describes the hundred languages of children as symbolic languages they use to express their own knowledge and desires through artwork, conversation, early writing, dramatic play, music, dance, and other outlets. Fostering and supporting these languages goes hand in hand with supporting playful learning in early childhood education. When considering playful STEAM explorations, a Reggio Emilia environment helps to foster creativity and curiosity. This approach emphasizes the importance of the learning environment and encourages children to express themselves in multiple ways, fostering creativity and critical thinking in STEAM education. In Reggio Emilia–inspired learning settings, educators emphasize using materials and activities that provoke investigation and group learning—all key components of building confidence and competence in STEAM. For example, a Reggio-inspired preschool classroom may have a dedicated "science corner" or a similar dedicated environment with welcoming furniture arranged to promote group conversations and collaborative learning. This corner would likely include sensory, hands-on materials as well as tools to spark inquiry like magnets, magnifying glasses, and microscopes.

Montessori Method

Although a Montessori classroom might look to an untrained eye like a Reggio Emilia–inspired classroom, with its emphasis on neatness, child-accessible tools, and beauty, the deep philosophical differences are incorporated into almost every aspect of the environment. An overly simplistic comparison might connect Montessori with math and Reggio Emilia with art, but the differences run deeper than subject emphasis. Montessori environments are rooted in a belief that children's learning must be self-motivated and requires organized, sequential opportunities to cater to their predictable developmental progress. Where Reggio Emilia emphasizes collective community, including adults and institutions beyond the school, Montessori stresses the individuality and responsibility of each student to their classroom community.

Created by Dr. Maria Montessori over a century ago, the Montessori teaching method focuses on a child's natural inclination to learn (American Montessori Society, 2013; Montessori, 1912). In this environment, a teacher's role is to provide developmentally appropriate materials and give students the freedom to explore their personal interests. Teachers do not direct learning but respect children's efforts toward independent mastery (American Montessori Society, 2013; Montessori, 1912).

One of the defining features of the Montessori approach is that students stay in their respective classrooms for multiple years, giving them the opportunity to form close relationships with both their fellow students and their teacher (American Montessori Society, 2013; Lillard, 2010; Montessori, 1912). According to Montessori (1912), children's natural tendencies unfold when they are in these specially designed multiage environments. In this type of setting, collaboration plays a large role in the classroom to foster a sense of community among students.

Montessori classrooms are also known for the use of "beautiful objects" and manipulatives such as glass beads, metal, and wicker (American Montessori Society, 2013; Lillard, 2010). These materials are often used for counting, forming words, or playing games. This type of object-based learning has been associated with better learning outcomes and fostering cognitive development skills in young children (Glenberg et al., 2004; Montie et al., 2006). Montessori teachers demonstrate handling these fragile materials slowly and respectfully so that children naturally sense something magical about learning with them (American Montessori Society, 2013).

But a Montessori approach is so much more than just materials. Like STEAM, it is a *process* and *method* of teaching and learning. STEAM through a Montessori lens gives students the tools they need to learn while placing ownership of learning on the student. Giving students ownership of their learning is a concept we'll return to throughout this book and is a critical piece of supporting young children's confidence and competence in STEAM domains—and thus, a critical piece of supporting their STEAM identity.

* * *

Playful STEAM, much like the Montessori approach, is about doing, building, and creating in authentic contexts. A Montessori approach to STEAM will focus on solving real-world problems in a project-based, experiential learning environment, often through exploring practical life activities. An example of a Montessori-style STEAM project might include planting a garden to create a useful solution for an area of the school's outdoor environment that is not being used. This would entail planting seeds and observing their growth from seeds, to sprouts, to leaves and flowers, then caring for the flowers over time and through different seasons. This type of Montessori project focuses on self-directed, hands-on learning that supports the development of independence and problem-solving skills crucial for STEAM learning.

Loose Parts Theory and Affordance Theory

The theory of loose parts was established in 1972 by architect Simon Nicholson, and it centers on the idea that loose parts (i.e., materials that can be moved around, designed and redesigned, and tinkered with) create infinitely more opportunities for creative engagement than static materials and environments. This theory posits that, in a nutshell, more materials lead to more interactions. As an architect, Nicholson developed this theory around envisioning the design of playgrounds and schools, rethinking the static play equipment and environment and instead incorporating loose materials to engage children's natural creativity and inventiveness. As it relates to STEAM education, loose parts theory emphasizes that children can learn through play with everyday materials that can be moved around, altered, and redesigned (think beads, pipe cleaners, wooden blocks, and building bricks) to create games, build playhouses, or engage in solitary play.

Much like loose parts theory, affordance theory also illustrates the use of loose materials to foster creative thinking and learning. For example, affordance theory would state that when you offer common and flexible objects, such as cardboard boxes or plastic beads, children are apt to view them through the lens of what they can "afford" to play—what they can do or be—rather than in the context of their intended purpose. For example, a cardboard box is a simple object whose function is to contain other materials. But young children famously understand the "affordances" of a cardboard box for imaginative play: containing space; dividing inside from outside; creating shadow and light; a tool for standing, balancing, crawling, hiding; and countless other creative purposes (Casey et al., 2016). In fact, long-term studies of elementary-aged students with access to different playgrounds found that offering cheap and simple tools like buckets and crates was more effective at supporting creativity, social play, and problem-solving skills compared to expensive play equipment (Science Daily, 2014).

Loose parts encourage imaginative play and creative problem-solving—both of which are essential components of STEAM education. We will draw on the theory of loose parts and affordance theory in the curricular examples and approaches presented throughout this book

PLAYPENS VS. PLAYGROUNDS

We have discussed materials, environments, and the teacher's role through various approaches and theories of learning in the early childhood years. We connect these theories to STEAM specifically by building on the hands-on, child-directed, open-ended environments described throughout this chapter. Research has shown that many of children's best learning experiences come when they are engaged not simply in interacting with materials but in designing, creating, and inventing with them (Papert, 1980; Resnick, 2006).

A final theoretical framework that we situate our examples and approaches in is the Positive Technological Development framework first introduced in Chapter 2. The PTD framework guides the development, implementation, and evaluation of educational programs that use new technologies to promote learning as an aspect of positive youth development through promoting "six C's" when using technology: content creation, creativity, communication, collaboration, community building and choices of conduct. We build on Bers's six C's and argue that these positive behaviors can also be fostered during technology-free STEAM learning and play.

Bers (2020) also presents the metaphor of "playgrounds versus playpens" to distinguish between different types of playful learning experiences that are common in early childhood environments. Playpens, as Bers notes, keep children safe, but they also keep them isolated. They limit their options, eliminate creative opportunities, cut off any chance of real exploration, and erect physical barriers to collaboration with other children. Playgrounds, on the other hand, allow children much more autonomy and choice. Playgrounds encourage kids to explore and play together, and to create new games alone or collaborate with their peers (Bers, 2020).

Bers argues that children need more technological experiences that resemble the playground environment—experiences where children have autonomy, express creativity, explore their curiosities, and collaborate with peers. We expand this concept to relate to all STEM/STEAM learning experiences, those including both technology and unplugged experiences. This metaphor of playpen vs. playground STEAM learning environments is something we will return to time and time again throughout this book.

CONCLUDING THOUGHTS

There is not one "right" approach, theory, environment, or strategy when it comes to early learning and play. Integrating diverse pedagogical strategies helps create a dynamic and responsive STEAM curriculum that meets the needs of all learners. We encourage educators reading this book to become inspired by the different approaches described throughout this chapter and think about how combining elements from various pedagogies may be especially effective for encouraging student agency and inquiry-based learning. A well-rounded approach to STEAM education, rooted in multiple pedagogical traditions, equips students with the skills and mindset needed to thrive in a complex, rapidly changing world.

In Part III of this book, we present real-world examples of exemplary STEAM practices, offer success stories from diverse educational settings, and focus on the impact of integrated pedagogies on student outcomes. This is meant to provide valuable insights and inspiration for implementing effective STEAM practices in various educational contexts.

CHAPTER 6

Planning and Implementing STEAM in Formal Classroom Settings

This chapter aims to guide educators in designing and implementing standards-aligned curricula, lesson plans, and evaluation approaches that embody the Playful STEAM Learning Framework in formal classroom settings to foster creativity and critical thinking. We will focus on designing playful educational experiences for young children, emphasizing the importance of effective curriculum design and time management. While this book focuses on playful STEAM experiences for children ages 2–8, the current chapter will primarily focus on children ages 5–8 who are typically in formal learning settings (kindergarten–3rd grade). Most educational standards related to STEAM also generally begin at the kindergarten level. Upcoming chapters of this book, emphasizing informal learning settings and everyday play, will focus on the full 2–8-year age range, providing examples and strategies for our youngest learners who are not yet in kindergarten.

To begin, what do we mean by "formal" classroom settings? Formal learning environments vary widely but are often characterized by a structured and scheduled approach to education, with activities organized according to a curriculum, led by certified educators in institutional settings to meet specific learning objectives. Student progress along these objectives is usually assessed, although assessment approaches vary widely and encompass a range of interpretive formats for this young age group. Formal learning environments may include public and private preschools, kindergartens, elementary schools, day cares with educational programs, alternative schools (e.g., Waldorf, charter, magnet, Montessori), and early childhood education programs within community centers. This chapter will focus on this type of learning environment and address classroom settings and the unique opportunities (and constraints) for STEAM learning that come with a full-year curriculum-aligned learning environment. In the next chapter, we will delve into strategies and approaches for the world of informal STEAM learning (e.g., museums, camps, after-school programs, informal day care settings, home settings, and more); and in Chapter 8, we will explore supporting STEAM in everyday play.

STEAM CURRICULUM AND LESSONS

The Playful STEAM Learning Framework, introduced in Part I of this book, describes play as an essential part of learning during the foundational early childhood and early elementary school years. But unstructured play has been notably absent in formal learning settings, particularly beginning in kindergarten, in recent years. This is in part due to growing pressure of frameworks, standards, and standardized testing in public schools. We will offer strategies for planning curricula that can meet these guidelines while also offering opportunities for curiosity-based, child-led, and authentic play.

Before diving into planning strategies, it's important to remember the differences between a curriculum and a lesson plan, which are commonly confused or used interchangeably in practice even by very experienced researchers and educators. Table 6.1 describes these differences in detail. Principally, the curriculum serves as a comprehensive guide for the overall educational program, while a lesson plan provides the detailed steps needed to deliver specific instructional activities within that broader framework. Another way to think of these structures is that a curriculum describes the handful of major learning outcomes for a student during their entire time in a grade, while the lesson plans build the many small and incremental, but necessary, steps in their learning toward achieving mastery of the few big ideas outlined within their curriculum.

Table 6.1. Key Differences Between Curriculum and Lesson Plan

	Curriculum	Lesson Plan
Definition	A structured framework that outlines the educational goals in terms of knowledge (content, skills, and attitudes), learning experiences, and evaluation measures for a specific course, age level, or educational program over a defined period (Print, 1993).	A detailed, step-by-step guide created by an educator to deliver a specific lesson or series of lessons within a shorter time frame (such as a single class period or a week) (Farrell, 2002).
Scope	Broad, encompassing the entire span of the educational program, outlining what students are expected to learn and how their learning will be assessed (Ornstein & Hunkins, 2018).	Narrow, detailing the hourly, daily, or weekly planned instructional activities, designed to facilitate specific educational objectives (Richards & Bohlke, 2011).

(continued)

Table 6.1. (*continued*)

	Curriculum	Lesson Plan
Components	Includes subject matter content, broad learning targets, instructional methods, student evaluation approaches, and relevant educational standards or benchmarks (Posner, 2004).	Includes specific learning objectives for the lesson, instructional activities, materials needed, time allocation, and assessment methods for evaluating student learning or performance outcomes during or after the lesson (Reed & Michaud, 2010).
Purpose	Provides a comprehensive guide for educators to convey the meaning of the educational pursuit and to ensure consistency and coherence in teaching, aligning with educational standards and goals at a school, district, or national level (Glatthorn et al., 2018).	Provides a clear, stepwise, practical guide for teachers to effectively deliver content, engage students, and assess their understanding in a structured and organized manner (Kyriacou, 2007).
Example	A yearlong elementary science curriculum that outlines all of the core topics (e.g., ecosystems, weather, simple machines, etc.), learning goals (e.g., broad science skills and practices), and culminating assessment methods (e.g., final project and written exam) for each grade.	A 1-hour lesson plan for a 2nd-grade science class on the water cycle, detailing student performance objectives (e.g., students will be able to describe the stages of the water cycle), instructional activities (e.g., teacher demonstration, group discussion, student-led hands-on experiment), materials needed (e.g., water, heat source, containers), and assessment methods (e.g., student drawings in lab notebook and explanations in group discussion of the water cycle stages).

A well-designed STEAM curriculum aligns with educational standards while promoting exploratory play and hands-on learning. A key element of STEAM curriculum, as opposed to just a stand-alone math or science curriculum, is the focus on interdisciplinary learning. A successful STEAM curriculum should encourage interdisciplinary learning by drawing on knowledge and skills from various domains. For example, students may apply math skills about counting and estimation to a computer science project on coding. Or they may utilize arts and crafts skills and practices to design a diorama as part of a science project.

Authentic play experiences, rooted in real-world relevance, are another key element of the Playful STEAM Learning Framework. When planning the scope of a STEAM curriculum, educators should plan content that encourages children to see the real-world applications of the projects and activities they are creating. At the early childhood level, this may include engineering design projects that focus on improving your classroom, growing a garden for school beautification while learning about the life cycle of plants, or building a model bridge and then learning about famous bridges in your state.

ALIGNING PLAYFUL STEAM CURRICULUM WITH STANDARDS AND FRAMEWORKS

How do the key elements of quality STEAM curriculum and lessons fit into existing frameworks and standards? Educational standards and frameworks provide a foundation for what students are expected to learn at each grade level, ensuring that educators across the state—or country, in the case of national frameworks—have clearly defined and shared goals to guide their classroom practice. From the widely adopted Common Core standards to state-specific frameworks and standards, these guidelines were developed to help educators support improved student learning and achievement. Educational standards also provide guidelines and benchmarks for teaching and learning that aim to support equitable and quality education for all students. In addition to state-specific standards where you are located, many of the standards that you may draw on when developing STEAM curriculum are summarized in Table 6.2.

The Next Generation Science Standards (NGSS) are a great source of guidance when it comes to developing integrated STEAM curricula. NGSS are K–12 science content standards that set expectations for what students should know and be able to do. A goal for developing the NGSS was to create a set of research-based, up-to-date K–12 science standards to improve science education for all students. Every NGSS standard has three dimensions: disciplinary core ideas (content), scientific and engineering practices, and crosscutting concepts. The integration of content and application as described in the NGSS standards reflects how science and engineering are practiced in the real world, and often describe connections to other disciplines as well, including writing, reading, and math.

Playful STEAM learning can blend naturally with NGSS by supporting children to learn by engaging in meaningful projects, with open-ended hands-on exploration—not just the rote memorization of facts. The goal of STEAM instruction guided by NGSS is for children to become creative problem-solvers who can understand and apply the science concepts they learn.

Table 6.2. Standards and Frameworks With STEAM Connections

Standards/ Frameworks	Description	STEAM Connection
Next Generation Science Standards (NGSS)	K–12 science content standards that set expectations for what students should know and be able to do. The NGSS were developed by states to improve science education for all students.	S—Science
Common Core Standards	Common Core math and English language arts standards explain what students should know and be able to do by the end of each grade level from K–12.	A—Arts (Language Arts) M—Math
K–12 Computer Science Framework	The K–12 Computer Science Framework illuminates the big ideas of computer science through a lens of concepts (i.e., what students should know) and practices (i.e., what students should do).	T—Technology
Computer Science Teacher's Association (CSTA) K–12 Computer Science Standards	These standards delineate a core set of learning objectives designed to provide the foundation for a complete computer science curriculum and its implementation at the K–12 level.	T—Technology
International Society for Technology in Education (ISTE) Standards	The ISTE standards provide the competencies for learning, teaching, and leading with technology, and are a comprehensive road map for the effective use of technology in schools worldwide.	T—Technology
National Core Arts Standards	A conceptual framework for arts learning that outlines the philosophy, primary goals, dynamic processes, structures, and outcomes that shape student learning and achievement in dance, media arts, music, theatre, and visual arts.	A—Arts

Whether drawing on NGSS or another set of standards, there are a few steps we recommend educators move through when working to develop a standards-aligned STEAM curriculum for early learners:

- **Learn the standards:** Fully explore the standards for your age range that you will align your curriculum with to make sure you understand them.

- **Review your current/past curriculum:** Review your current (or previously implemented) curriculum to see how well it aligns with the standards and identify any strengths or weaknesses. If you are using NGSS, you can use the NGSS website, app, or the NGSS alignment tool to compare your curriculum with the standards and see how well your content matches up.
- **Make meaningful changes:** Make meaningful changes to better align with the standards you are using as your guide. This may mean adapting a prior curriculum—or creating and adopting something completely new!
- **Center your students:** Consider the specific needs of your learners, and identify any special arrangements or adaptations your curriculum may need to put their unique needs first. This may mean returning to the previous step of making meaningful changes to your curriculum.
- **Identify evaluation metrics:** This about how you will monitor and assess your students' learning, progress toward their learning goals, and determine how you will provide them with meaningful feedback. Additionally, come up with a plan for reflecting on and evaluating your own teaching practice. This may involve self-evaluation and may also involve seeking feedback from colleagues.

Importantly, standards give us a goal for what students should be able to do in practice, as evidence of their progressive development of a mature mental model of a subject area. The language of students "understanding" a topic is useful in the abstract, but as a curricular or lesson goal, it is not possible to actually capture student knowledge without somehow being able to read their thoughts. Instead, evaluation and learning objectives should focus on observable, measurable, and concrete student performance benchmarks. For example, observable performance benchmarks might include whether a child can classify objects based on their properties or create a functional code for their robot using a very simple programming language. In the elementary years, students' ability to form mental models may outpace their ability to communicate or illustrate them (e.g., Vosniadou, 1994), and project- and observation-based assessment measures are a popular method of summative assessment in STEAM lesson planning for this reason.

PLAY-BASED STEAM LEARNING IN FORMAL CLASSROOMS

We have discussed creating a standards-aligned STEAM curriculum, but what about a *playful* STEAM curriculum? The loss of play-based learning for our youngest formal education students (kindergarteners) has been an issue since the implementation of the 2001 No Child Left Behind (NCLB)

Act, which marked an increase in scripted curricula, standardized paper-based testing, and scrutiny of teaching practices and student achievement. While the purpose of NCLB was to increase the academic achievement for all students, the associated increase in mandated standardized testing that came along with it put new pressure on teachers and young students alike.

We know from the research summarized in Part I of this book how essential play is to learning, especially when it comes to STEAM, in the foundational early childhood years. However, the reality is that many standards that guide educators' curriculum and teaching practices do not fit well within a play-based learning framework. For example, standards that focus on discrete, measurable skills that are gained through memorization and/or repetition may align better with a direct-instruction approach rather than a play-based approach. But when it comes to many STEAM standards that focus on approaches, mindsets, and concepts that are learned best through hands-on projects, playful learning approaches can be a perfect fit.

Truly play-based learning is fading even at the preschool, prekindergarten, and kindergarten levels. In elementary school classrooms (1st grade and up), it is very rare to find. However, some notable examples of schools throughout the United States have demonstrated the powerful benefits of a play-based approach even in the upper elementary years. For example, in 2021, the Oklahoma legislature passed a law that encourages the use of play in pre-K through 3rd-grade classrooms. Now, the Oklahoma City School District is among the few in the United States that has been experimenting with increased playtime for children as old as 8–9 years (Gilreath, 2022). *In these Oklahoma City schools, play-based learning sometimes involves moving through hands-on centers to explore concepts like static electricity or using wooden construction toys to make a model of the solar system or even freely choosing materials to play with while reflecting on a specific prompt from their teacher (Gilreath, 2022).*

In Watertown, New York, educators have been teaching through play in pre-K and kindergarten for years, but have only recently shifted to encouraging play for older elementary students as well (Gilreath, 2022). In other schools, including some in Austin, Texas, elementary teachers are trained to use LEGO Education products as a play-based learning tool during class time. Manor Independent School District, a district near Austin, launched a growing robotics program a decade ago in an attempt to bring more playful learning to students in the early years of elementary school (Gilreath, 2022). For several years, robotics was mostly confined to after-school programs—which is still true of many robotics and engineering initiatives throughout the United States. These tools provide a unique opportunity for playful learning of engineering and computer science content. We will delve more into using robotics and coding as a tool for play-based STEAM learning in Part III of this book.

We know that not all educators will have the luxury of school support, budget, and time to create elementary school learning environments that encourage a fully play-based approach, particularly for children in grades 2–3. However, there are ways to ensure that your STEAM curricular content includes play-based learning opportunities regularly throughout the day and year. When planning STEAM lessons that align with standards while also including opportunities for learning through play, educators can focus on designing learning experiences that include the following:

- **Choices for students:** Provide students with opportunities to guide their learning and exploration, even within the confines of a specific topic or concept area that is dictated by standards.
- **Hands-on:** As much as possible, create hands-on opportunities to explore concepts and gain STEAM skills.
- **Create "playground" learning experiences:** Recall the "playground vs. playpens" (Bers, 2020) metaphor for playful learning that we described earlier in this book, and think about providing students with open-ended "playground" opportunities rather than solely restricted, step-by-step "playpen" activities. This will add to the child-led, joyful, and playful experience for your young learners.
- **Create open-ended opportunities:** Budget time for students to test their skills and make discoveries related to curricular content through open-ended play and experimentation. This might happen by setting out specific materials and prompts that students can freely explore during centers, outside during recess, or during other unstructured moments in the day.

STRATEGIES: IMPLEMENTING PLAYFUL STEAM LESSONS IN THE CLASSROOM

Despite the confines of the formal school day, it *is* possible to create an organized and resource-rich environment that supports effective STEAM learning and encourages student participation and play. A few strategies to help with this include:

- **Creating a STEAM-friendly classroom environment:** Create a STEAM-friendly classroom that includes developmentally appropriate STEAM books (nonfiction and fiction) featuring diverse individuals, STEAM materials and resources that are organized for easy access, and tools and materials that are safe for children to explore on their own without heavy adult instruction. These books and materials can be offered during centers, story time, times when children finish work early, or other times throughout the day that are set aside for unstructured learning and play. If students feel overwhelmed by the free-choice nature of these environments or materials (as sometimes happens with older students who have not much experience with free play in school settings), you might provide simple and open-ended prompts to inspire low-stakes, curiosity-based play.

- **Managing time effectively to balance instruction and play:** When it comes to STEAM curricula, we encourage you to build in time for free play and exploration to help students solidify concepts through their own hands-on play and child-led discoveries. This means that if you are planning a 10-hour coding curriculum, for example, plan for at least 1 hour of that to include open-ended experimentation with your coding interface without a specific teacher-directed goal. This might mean the last 15 minutes of each coding lesson is set aside for this free play, or it might mean your coding interface is offered during centers or another time throughout the day. By writing in and planning for play, you set yourself up for success when it comes to implementation. Often, this predictable and scheduled outlet for creative, unstructured play also supports students who tend toward behavioral or socio-emotional issues as a result of feeling overwhelmed by classroom expectations.
- **Leverage your community outside the school:** Play-based STEAM learning can be messy, require additional hands-on materials, and be chaotic to set up, clean up, and facilitate. These projects are the perfect opportunity to support the home–school connection by encouraging families and other caregivers to volunteer, send in materials, or help in other ways. You can also leverage the community outside beyond students' families with contacts through your city, local museums, universities, and more.

We know there are many factors that go into devising an effective lesson plan and curriculum, especially when integrating moments for play. We encourage you to use the Playful STEAM Lesson Planning Sheet (Appendix B) and Playful STEAM Curriculum Planning Sheet (Appendix C) to further map out the details of your effective playful STEAM learning plan. These appendixes are also available online (https://www.tcpress.com/playful-steam-learning-in-the-early-years-9780807787083) in a format that is ideal for printing.

EVALUATION: APPROACHES FOR CAPTURING STEAM LEARNING

We cannot let a chapter on STEAM in formal classroom settings go by without touching on evaluation. One of the hesitations many educators and school administrators feel when moving toward increased play in the classroom is that student learning and achievement are sacrificed. By using diverse assessment methods, you will be able to capture a comprehensive understanding of student progress and areas for growth. In this section, we will summarize a few approaches you may take, and we encourage you to think about assessment further when planning your curriculum and lessons using the planning sheets found in the appendixes of this book available online.

Formative Assessments. Formative assessment refers to assessments used to identify struggles and learning gaps throughout a lesson or longer curriculum in order to identify and close those gaps. Formative assessment includes daily "checks for understanding" that help you—and your students—monitor and take ownership of the learning process. You can identify specific checks for understanding that are important to you or specifically related to your STEAM lesson content. We typically use the following questions as a starting point: What are students learning? What new skills or understanding have they gained? What skills, practices, or behaviors can show us that they are thinking about these ideas in the ways we expect? These questions can be answered in a variety of ways that are "low stakes" for students and allow educators to get a sense of students' knowledge of a topic before waiting for a final project, portfolio, or exam. Some easy-to-implement formative assessments include:

- **Entrance and Exit Questions:** Students answer a question when entering the classroom and exiting the classroom so you can get a quick idea of whether they understand a particular concept.
- **Positive, Negative, Interesting:** Wrap up a STEAM lesson by having students share things about the lesson that they found positive, negative, and/or interesting. For younger children, you may have them share "Apples and Onions"—their highlights/favorite parts of the lesson and their least favorite elements.
- **Newspaper Headline:** Have students summarize the main concept of the lesson in a concise newspaper headline.

These formative assessments can be implemented individually, written on paper, as a group discussion, individual discussion, or in other ways to meet the needs of your students and classrooms.

Summative Assessments. Unlike formative assessments, which help you gauge student learning and make shifts as you progress throughout a curriculum, summative assessments evaluate student learning and knowledge at the end of a lesson or unit. Depending on the grade level you teach or the structure of your school, these assessments may go along with formally graded assessments. When formative and summative assessments are planned in conjunction, they can be used together throughout a STEAM unit to best support students' learning. Especially for older students, summative assessments traditionally include tests or exams. However, other summative assessments that tie nicely with playful STEAM learning include:

- **Final projects:** Students' work on a STEAM topic culminates in a final project where they apply their knowledge and skills to a topic they are personally interested in.
- **Presentations and showcases:** Students present their learning in a presentation for classmates, peers, and family/friends. This can be done live and/or include video-recorded presentations that are more easily shared with family and friends.
- **Portfolios:** Students' work on a subject or project is compiled over a period of time so that iterative changes in their learning and development can be seen.

Other Assessment Techniques. Classroom observation is another tool that is particularly useful in play-based learning environments when teachers are in the role of facilitator/co-learner as opposed to a direct instructor. As students are playing and experimenting, educators can observe their actions and use open-ended questions to gain insight into their learning. When students face challenges, educators can provide hints, prompts, and nudges to foster deeper learning and discovery. During classroom observation, educators can also capture images, videos, and notes that can be used in portfolios or other summative evaluations later on.

As both a summative and a formative assessment technique, self-reflection and self-assessment can also engage students. How would they describe their learning and the skills they gained? Did they enjoy the content being explored? Did they build confidence? Depending on the age of your students, these reflections can happen through group discussions, drawings, or writing.

Lastly, consider regularly checking in and assessing not just students' mastery of concepts and skills but their overall attitudes, enjoyment, and experience. You may also wish to assess habits of learning like collaboration, teamwork, communication, and other areas that can flourish—or face roadblocks—throughout a STEAM curriculum.

CONCLUDING THOUGHTS

Formal classroom environments present unique challenges and benefits when implementing playful STEAM learning activities. Through careful planning, time management, and strategic use of formative and summative evaluation, educators can be successful and integrate fun and playful STEAM content that also prompts deep learning and mastery of skills in accordance with standards and frameworks. We encourage educators to utilize the planning sheets in Appendixes B and C of this book to further delve into planning and preparation for implementing play-based STEAM.

CHAPTER 7

Planning and Implementing STEAM in Informal Learning Settings

In the previous chapter, we explored strategies for implementing STEAM in formal learning settings, mainly kindergarten to 3rd-grade classrooms. While we often think of the sciences as a core component of formal learning (and they are), informal learning settings provide unique strategies for exploring STEAM concepts in ways that are hands-on and play-based, as well as low stakes, authentic, and slower paced. All of the strategies related to assessments and activity planning discussed in the previous chapter can also be adapted and used in informal learning settings, often with less importance placed on relating experiences to learning standards, frameworks, and testing. However, informal learning settings also provide their own opportunities and challenges when it comes to playful STEAM activities that warrant a dedicated chapter to explore.

But first, what do we mean by informal learning settings and opportunities? Informal learning opportunities refer to any learning that occurs outside of the formal classroom context. When thinking about young children, this can make up a significant portion of their time exploring and gaining new skills. In fact, preschool children spend *more than 80% of their waking hours* engaging in informal learning experiences outside of school settings (Alexandre et al., 2022; Bell et al., 2009; Kornelaki & Plakitsi, 2018; Osborne & Dillon, 2007). This type of learning may occur in a variety of places including museums and other cultural institutions, after-school clubs, camps, and at home during everyday activities, such as cooking, building with LEGOs, or playing with blocks and puzzles. For very young children, informal settings may also include informal child care settings (e.g., home day cares) depending on how the setting is structured.

Because of the many unique opportunities that informal settings provide, informal education is increasingly being targeted as part of a comprehensive effort to increase STEM engagement, stimulate and build interest, and support learning (Bell et al., 2009). Informal STEAM learning is typically characterized as social, playful, and engaging in ways that foster children's natural tendency to ask questions, explore, and experiment (Bell et al., 2009). The core qualities of informal learning—including free choice, being individually meaningful, and occurring within a social context—contribute to making informal learning especially unique and valuable when it comes to STEAM education. Moreover, early informal learning experiences have the potential to enhance children's readiness to engage in science learning in school and encourage lifelong STEAM pursuits.

As children get older and enter formal school settings, out-of-school time (OST) programs such as after-school programs, clubs, and camps become a major part of their playful learning experience. Therefore, it may not be surprising to learn that after-school programs are a major vehicle for increasing interest, confidence, and capacity in the sciences, particularly for historically excluded students (National Research Council, 2009). Effective after-school programs help broaden participation in STEAM in ways that directly align with the Playful STEAM Learning Framework by providing relevant, hands-on opportunities for youth to interact with relatable scientific role models, content knowledge, and resources (Coalition for Science After School, 2007).

THE BENEFITS OF INFORMAL STEAM

There are many benefits specific to exploring STEAM in informal learning settings. Research has found that participation in informal science activities fosters children's abilities of scientific reasoning and increases their commitment to science learning (Bell et al., 2009; Gerber et al., 2001). Informal learning environments may also increase students' interest in STEM and increase the chances they will pursue a STEM career (Kitchen et al., 2018; Mohr-Schroeder et al., 2014).

Whether it is choosing a camp, a club, or an out-of-school time class, informal learning opportunities also allow children (alongside their caregivers in the instance of very young children) to *choose* the content they want to engage with based on their own interests and curiosities. This means that children are engaging with content that is typically more personally meaningful and interesting to them than other classes they are assigned to throughout the formal learning day. Within the programs themselves, informal learning settings tend to embrace providing youth with choice. The free-choice aspect of informal learning settings provides a variety of entry points to learning, especially when thinking about broadening participation and reaching children with diverse backgrounds, interests, and levels of expertise (Falk & Dierking, 2010).

Students who struggle or appear uninterested in the sciences in formal school settings may have the most to gain from informal STEAM learning opportunities, which are often presented in more fun, approachable, and hands-on ways than in classroom contexts. Informal STEAM learning environments promote learning through real-world modeling and examples, making the learning that happens in these spaces more authentic and meaningful (Martin, 2004; Meredith, 2010; Popovic & Lederman, 2015). Therefore, it is not surprising that youth who consistently participate in informal STEAM activities generally report positive changes in their science-related attitudes, with the greatest gains being reported by those participating in programs that demonstrate the highest levels of quality in areas like inquiry, reflection, and relevance (Allen et al., 2017).

EXAMPLES OF PLAYFUL STEAM IN INFORMAL LEARNING SETTINGS

There are many ways to foster playful STEAM exploration and learning in informal learning settings, including drawing on resources provided by existing programs offered nationwide. We will provide a few examples of existing informal STEAM programs and initiatives offered nationally, along with ideas and examples of programs that can be developed and facilitated by individual groups, school districts, and communities. As you are reading about these programs, keep in mind that even though all are offered outside of the formal school day, they vary in terms of formality, structure, and how play-based they are.

FIRST LEGO League. The FIRST LEGO League is an example of a program that introduces STEAM content to children as young as 4 through fun and exciting hands-on learning. FIRST participants gain real-world problem-solving experience through a guided, global robotics program. There are three divisions of FIRST, with the first two (Discover and Explore) being designed for children 8 and under. FIRST Discover, designed for children ages 4–6, is a playful introductory program that ignites young students' natural curiosity and builds their habits of learning with hands-on activities using LEGO DUPLO bricks. Meanwhile in FIRST Explore, teams of students ages 6–10 focus on the fundamentals of engineering as they explore real-world problems, learn to design and code, and create unique solutions made with LEGO bricks and powered by LEGO Education SPIKE Essential robotics kits.

Science Olympiad. Founded in 1984, Science Olympiad is one of the biggest team-based STEM competitions in the nation, providing standards-based challenges to 6,300 teams at 425 tournaments in all 50 states. Beginning with kindergarten, there are opportunities to participate in the Science Olympiad. The Elementary Science Olympiad (ESO) is implemented differently at different locations, but all work under the unifying idea of children learning by doing science. ESO offers hands-on, inquiry-based activities that challenge students in grades K–6 to build their understanding of basic scientific concepts, like engineering design, and practices, like accurate measurement.

Girl Scouts. The Girl Scouts of the United States (GSUSA) offers opportunities for girls beginning in kindergarten to engage in fun, friendship, and hands-on learning activities. A key element of the GSUSA program is earning badges. Girl Scouts can earn badges by trying new skills and activities, and demonstrating their experiences to their troop leader. What does this all have to do with STEAM? Since 2015, GSUSA launched more than 100 new STEM programs, and Girl Scouts earned over 5 million STEM badges (Girl Scout Research Institute, 2022). In Girl Scouts, girls experience science, technology, engineering, and math through engaging activities that relate to their interests to impact the world. GSUSA programs give girls the training, mentoring, and hands-on experiences to help them understand the value of STEM/STEAM for bettering society and the options for their own related career paths. Girls see how STEM activities and careers are relevant to them through engaging activities, such as using shapes and numbers to create nature-inspired art in the Math in Nature badges (Girl Scout Research Institute, 2022).

Other Examples. Many schools, camps, libraries, and parks and recreation departments offer informal STEAM programs of their own creation, often drawing on the expertise and interests of their community members (parents, students, local professionals, and others). We, the authors of this book, spent much of our STEAM education careers teaching after-school robotics for local public schools, mixed-age "Saturday STEAM Classes" for community enrichment programs, and immersive coding and engineering summer camps offered through local universities (Strawhacker, 2020; Sullivan, 2019). Through these experiences, we saw firsthand the power of fun, hands-on, play-based STEAM explorations in an informal context. Without the typical constraints of the school day, students were free to make authentic discoveries on their own timetable, through guided prompts and scaffolding by adults. Table 7.1 provides examples of different types of

Table 7.1. Examples of Informal STEAM Programs

Program Example	Grade Level	Potential Setting
STEAM Story Time	Preschool or younger	Library or school setting
Parent & Me STEAM Playgroup	Preschool or younger	Library or museum
Saturday or Sunday STEAM Club	K–3	Library, school, museum
After-School Robotics Club	1–3	Parks and recreation department, library, school, privately owned space
Engineering, Space, or Math Camp	1–3	Library, school, museum, privately owned space
Girls Coding Club	1–3	Library, school, privately owned space

informal learning programs along with the grade level they would be most applicable to and potential settings in which these programs could be held.

COMMUNITY SCIENCE IN INFORMAL LEARNING SETTINGS

You may be interested in implementing an informal learning program but are not sure how to hone in on meaningful and authentic STEAM experiences. In this case, facilitating community or citizen science projects may be the right fit for you and the youth you serve. You may have heard terms like "community science," "citizen science," or "participatory science" before, all of which became even more popularized in the United States during the recent 2024 solar eclipse. These are all terms that mean, in a nutshell, real science engagement that is possible because of interested people across the country, and even globally, crowdsourcing their observations and evidence. Community science is science that is open to all and involves curious people whose individual acts contribute to a collective impact that is accelerating scientific research, discoveries, and local actions that improve the world. With many resources and ways to get involved, community science is the perfect way to bring authentic science learning and exploration to an informal learning setting.

Community science allows everyone—including children—to contribute to REAL scientific research and discoveries. Through this type of science, everyone can help study the world around them and send in the data they collect to scientists. From sharing photos of nature to helping scientists document biodiversity, to browsing images on your computer to help speed up research about Alzheimer's disease, each of these acts of science is important. During the 2024 total solar eclipse, for example, many people nationwide (both in and outside the eclipse path of totality) joined NASA to learn more about our sun and Earth and the effects of a total solar eclipse through community science projects.

Community science projects are the perfect way to engage young children in science in meaningful and authentic ways in a variety of informal learning settings. Visit Appendix D available online to learn more about community science resources and how you can bring these projects to your informal learning setting,

STRATEGIES FOR ALIGNING INFORMAL STEAM WITH THE PLAYFUL STEAM LEARNING FRAMEWORK

As we have discussed so far in this chapter, in many ways informal learning settings more readily align with the Playful STEAM Learning Framework described in Part I of this book than with formal learning programs. Table 7.2 demonstrates how the four pillars of the Playful STEAM framework

Table 7.2. The Playful STEAM Learning Framework in Informal Learning Settings

	P—Persevering through hard fun	L—Listening to children's ideas	A—Actively supporting inclusion	Y—Saying Yes to open-ended sensory play
In Practice in Informal STEAM Settings	Educators choose projects, materials, and activities that are sufficiently difficult for children.	Educators offer opportunities for choice. Educators support youth voice in selection and implementation of activities.	Programs develop advertising in order to reach a wide range of interested children. Programs are designed to be culturally, economically, geographically, and otherwise accessible to diverse learners. Logistics such as cost, transportation, and so on are considered.	Educators offer many opportunities for hands-on learning. Educators offer sensory experiences that may or may not have a direct goal or learning objective at the start.

(persevering through hard fun, listening to children's ideas, actively supporting inclusion, and saying yes to open-ended sensory play) can be put into practice by educators in informal learning settings.

There are also challenges to implementing quality STEAM in informal learning, which are not as much of an issue in formal learning settings, that are worth noting. For example, many informal learning programs may struggle with insufficient educator preparation (or even science or math anxiety) when it comes to STEAM, economic constraints that limit access to resources and enrichment programs, or issues with recruitment of students to participate in out-of-school-time STEAM programs. When you are actually implementing them, informal STEAM programs may not have the resources for program evaluation or student assessment, or you may have difficulty implementing a longer-scale STEAM project due to more changes in who attends day to day and week to week than a formal school program would have. We have included a planning sheet in Appendix C of this book to help educators and program administrators consider and plan for the unique challenges and affordances of informal learning settings when developing

STEAM programs. This planning sheet is also available in a format ideal for printing online at https://www.tcpress.com/playful-steam-learning-in-the-early-years-9780807787083.

CONCLUDING THOUGHTS

Regardless of whether STEAM programming is created for formal or informal learning environments, experiences created for young children must be engaging and offer opportunities for learning through play. It is important to note that formal and informal STEAM may have different learning goals (and outcomes) from one another—and that is okay! We know that children need *both* formal and informal learning experiences to gain skills and knowledge, particularly when it comes to the sciences. To illustrate this, let's return to the example of playing with slime presented in Chapter 2 in the following three playful STEAM learning vignettes.

Example 1: Making Slime in a 2nd-Grade Classroom

Over the course of the past week, 2nd-graders in Mrs. Santiago's science class have been learning about liquids, solids, and gases. Today, they are told they are going to make something that has the properties of both a liquid and a solid. Mrs. Santiago planned this lesson in accordance with NGSS science standards (specifically, 2-PS1-1: Plan and conduct an investigation to describe and classify different kinds of materials by their observable properties). In groups of two, children make slime using premeasured glue, baking soda, and contact lens solution. They mix their slime in large ziplock bags to contain mess as much as possible. Mrs. Santiago walks around to monitor students to make sure they are mixing their ingredients correctly. Students are given time to play, squeeze, and explore their slime bags. Then they are given worksheets to record their observations about the properties of the slime, and they participate in a full-class discussion about their observations. The bags of slime are put away in the classroom for use in centers and free-choice periods.

Students are disappointed when it is time to clean up the slime. A few grumble that they didn't have enough time to play with their slime, but Mrs. Santiago reminds them that the bags of slime are available to use again during free-choice periods. She asks her students if they would like to explore slime-making again in the future, and they excitedly say yes. Building on their excitement around slime, Mrs. Santiago plans another experiment for her class to do the following week. This time, they build on their prior knowledge of slime with a new challenge: to explore different formulas for slime using different amounts of contact lens solution. They observe differences in their slime's properties based on the amount of contact lens solution added and record their hypotheses and observations on a worksheet. Mrs. Santiago uses the worksheets to help assess each student's knowledge of experimental design and ability to make scientific observations.

Example 2: Making Slime at an After-School Science Club

Mixed-age students from grades 1-3 at Canyon Elementary School gather in Room 3 for their After-School Science Club. Today, they are making slime! There are two educators facilitating this club, Ms. Lindsey and Ms. Reyna, both of whom are parents to students in the class. The students are excited and full of energy after a long school day. Ms. Lindsey helps arrange the children into groups of four, while Ms. Reyna distributes premeasured materials for making slime (glue, baking soda, and contact lens solution). The groups work together mixing slime in large bowls. Ms. Reyna and Ms. Lindsey walk around prompting students to describe how their slime feels and looks. Ms. Lindsey asks, "Does your slime act more like a liquid or a solid?" There is some discussion of their observations, but they can tell their students are mostly engaged by squeezing, playing, and exploring their slime. While Ms. Reyna and Ms. Lindsey had a book they wanted to read aloud about the properties of slime, and what a non-Newtonian fluid is, they decide to skip it in order to give the students more time to play with their slime creations. Instead, the teachers walk from table to table offering additional mix-ins for the slimes including glitter, food coloring drops, scents, and plastic gems for the groups to personalize their slime. They take pictures to document each group's slime creation.

After-School Science Club is only 1 hour, once a week and the time goes by quickly. When it is time to clean up, Ms. Reyna helps each student wash their hands and pack up a little bit of slime into a small ziplock bag to take home. Ms. Lindsey puts a handout with a slime recipe they can try at home along with facts about slime and questions that parents/caregivers can ask their children about today's slime creation into each student's backpack.

Example 3: Making Slime at Home With a Preschooler

Stephanie, age 3, is excited to make slime with her dad! Working together in the kitchen, they mix together glue, contact lens solution, baking soda, and food coloring of Stephanie's choice (pink) in a large bowl. Once the slime is sufficiently mixed, Stephanie's dad transfers it to a plastic tray for her to play with. She plays with the slime while her dad cleans up the kitchen. Periodically, her dad asks her questions like "what does the slime feel like?" and "how does the slime move?" and "do you think this slime is any different from your Play-Doh?"

Stephanie says her slime feels like cupcake batter, and she engages in imaginary play with her slime, pretending she is a chef baking cupcakes.

Her dad gives her an old cupcake pan to play with. Once Stephanie is bored playing with the slime, her dad helps her clean it up, and they store it in a large ziplock bag to explore again another day.

Reflecting on the vignettes presented in this chapter, or on any STEAM activity observation from your own experience, we encourage you to think about the following questions:

- What do you think were the learning goals of each of these situations?
- How (or did) the adults in each situation incorporate play in different ways?
- How did each of the adults encourage choice and meet the needs of their learners?
- What are the different challenges presented by each of these situations?
- What are the benefits of each of these situations?
- What (if anything) would you do differently if you were an educator in one of these situations?

We hope you take away from these vignettes that no setting will ever be perfect and that it may be difficult to always hit on all aspects of the Playful STEAM Learning Framework. On the other hand, there is value (visible in children's joy and engagement, even without taking into consideration any other form of assessment) in implementing sensory STEAM play regardless of the early education setting you are in.

Are you ready to start planning for screen-free STEAM play for your learning settings? Parts III and IV of this book will introduce you to a variety of experiences, tools, and screen-free technologies that can be used to foster playful STEAM learning in different settings and situations.

Part III

LOW-TECH AND NO-TECH STEAM EXPERIENCES

CHAPTER 8

Integrating STEAM Into Everyday Play

STEAM naturally fits into many different playful learning scenarios that young children already engage in each day. From toys to puzzles, to board games, to imaginary play, there is a place for STEAM learning and exploration in all of the different types of play that young children enjoy. This chapter will provide an overview of how we can effectively foster STEAM learning in everyday play, including how educators can foster STEAM habits of mind like question-asking, curiosity, and authentic problem-solving as part of this play. Then, in Chapters 9 through 11, we will explore specific types of play and play environments including outdoor play, makerspaces, messy play, dramatic play, and more.

First, let's recall some of the characteristics of young children's play discussed in Part I. We explained that play is not one specific activity but a state of mind, more like a motivation or a mental attitude (Brown & Vaughan, 2009; Gray, 2013). Children's play can be guided or exploratory, social or independent, object-based or imaginative, but all play shares a few key components—most importantly that it is, well, FUN. Play is only play if it is pleasurable and enjoyable for the player, creating a feedback loop that spurs continuous engagement in the activity. That does not mean play can't include challenges (we talk about "hard fun" a lot in this book), but it *must* be enjoyable to be considered play.

Early childhood educators can facilitate play in different ways, depending on their setting. For example, an elementary school teacher might incorporate play by introducing games to review concepts. A preschool teacher may reserve time for open-ended play with different thematic materials each day before morning circle time. A parent may give kids freedom to play with toys in the playroom while they get chores and household tasks done. All of these approaches allow kids to engage in play in different ways.

MEANINGFUL PROMPTS FOR CHILD-LED STEAM PLAY

Whether you are designing a classroom space, a playroom, or an informal learning area, there are simple ways to include materials to prompt STEAM skills and exploration in child-led everyday play. In Table 8.1 we break down each area of S-T-E-A-M with examples of toys, tools, and products that can be included to prompt playful STEAM learning. In line with the screen-free focus of the Playful STEAM Learning Framework, we will highlight materials that can support screen-free STEAM play, including in the

Table 8.1. Toys, Tools, and Materials to Prompt Play for Each Area of STEAM

STEAM Area	Examples of Toys, Tools, and Materials	Examples of Playful Learning
S—Science	Child-size lab coats, goggles, astronaut suits, and other dramatic play costumes; child-size science tools like beakers, pipettes, magnifying glasses, and a microscope	Children pretending they are scientists and using science language • *Ex: A child puts on a lab coat and announces, "I'm going to do an experiment! Come help me in my lab!"* Children exploring cause and effect • *Ex: A child tries to use a pipette at the water table to fill up a small beaker. At first, she can't figure out how to use the pipette. A friend shows her that you need to squeeze the pipette to fill it and then squeeze again to release the water. She tries again and sees that the process works.*
T—Technology	Screen-free programmable robots designed for young children, like the KIBO Robotics Kit or Bee-Bot; screen-free coding board games like Robot Turtles	Children discover foundational coding concepts (e.g., sequencing) through play • *Ex: When trying to get their KIBO robot to move, a child realizes they must scan the green block first and the red block last or their code doesn't work.*

(*continued*)

Table 8.1. (*continued*)

STEAM Area	Examples of Toys, Tools, and Materials	Examples of Playful Learning
E—Engineering	Blocks, LEGO, cardboard, measuring tape, rulers, gears, child-friendly tools for building and construction	Children engaging in testing and improving their designs and structures • *Ex: When a child is trying to make a tower that is taller than her doll, her block tower falls down multiple times. She eventually realizes that if she creates a wider base, her tower is sturdier.*
A—Art	Open-ended arts and craft materials like crayons, paint, paper, pipe cleaners, tape, clay, and more; dramatic play materials like costumes and puppets; child-size musical instruments	Children explore fine art techniques and cause and effect • *Ex: A child making a finger painting explores what happens when red and yellow are mixed together. They made orange! The child goes on to try mixing other colors together to see what else they can create.*
M—Mathematics	Math manipulatives and toys like beads, blocks, counters, dice, fraction tiles, pattern blocks, dominoes, pretend money, shape blocks, and more	Children engage in a game of imaginary play running a restaurant, and they explore counting using pretend money • *Ex: Children set up a pretend restaurant. The child pretending to be a waiter gives the child pretending to be a customer a bill for the meal. The children explore counting by going through their play money to pay the correct amount for the bill.*

area of "T" (technology). This is by no means a comprehensive list but rather starting ideas to see how the addition of a few meaningful materials may prompt STEAM learning through play. Chapter 10, which discusses makerspaces, provides a more complete list of maker tools broken down by developmental level (toddler, preschooler, and early elementary students).

What is notable about open-ended, everyday play is the interdisciplinary learning and discovery that takes place. For example, when engaging in dramatic play pretending to run a restaurant, children may share ideas they know about food, cooking, and the roles and jobs of different people who work in a restaurant. Then they may explore math and counting when it comes to acting out being a customer paying for food. Children are also engaged in active communication, collaboration, and problem-solving when issues may occur like not having enough pretend money. With the addition of a few more meaningfully selected STEAM play props, this type of child-led play has boundless possibilities to grow and expand with the curiosity and imagination of the child.

STEAM BOARD GAMES

Another way to incorporate STEAM learning into everyday play is to offer STEAM-focused board games. Even without an explicit STEAM focus, board and card games are favorite playtime tools among educators and caregivers because they teach young children interpersonal skills like turn taking and patience. Classic games like Candyland and checkers teach children to remember simple rules and practice being a good winner and loser. Many board games also engage children in foundational skills like counting, number or color recognition, and practice with reading and language skills. Simple board and card games can be introduced in the preschool years, and as children get older, increasingly complex board games can be a fun way to engage in intergenerational play between younger children and older children or adults.

Research has demonstrated that board games can be an effective tool for supporting STEAM education and helping students reach a variety of outcomes, such as motivation, cognitive outcomes, and problem-solving skills (Cardinot & Fairfield, 2019; Cardinot et al., 2022; Chen et al., 2021; Hashim et al., 2024; Küçükşen Öner et al., 2024; Tsai et al., 2020; Vita-Barrull et al., 2023). Research suggests that integrating board games into STEAM education can improve student engagement and understanding of STEAM learning (Nguyen et al., 2024).

Table 8.2 provides examples of different types of board games that teach or reinforce STEAM skills or concepts, including technology-focused topics like coding. But how can educators implement board games in their learning settings? Board games naturally fit into informal learning or home settings (e.g., in a weekly Family Board Game night or as a choice during open-ended after-school care). They can be effective playful learning tools in formal classroom settings, too. In early elementary school, board games can be used to teach or practice skills from a range of subjects, including all the STEAM disciplines. For example, in mathematics, you can use the card game Uno for kindergarten and 1st-graders to practice number and color recognition, or Battleship to teach older elementary students about coordinates. Board games can be used to review key concepts, and teachers can even adapt board games by adding questions that tie curricular content to a game. For example, you can tape questions to the blocks in a game of Jenga or checkers to add a curricular element to traditional gameplay.

In addition to the newer STEAM-focused games described in Table 8.2, most traditional board games reinforce mathematics skills like counting or rely on reading skills to engage with gameplay. For example, games like Monopoly (or Monopoly Jr. for younger kids) are great for exploring math (specifically, financial concepts and money management) and include some reading as well. Whatever the concept you want to reinforce or teach, there is likely a board game (classic or new) that can help infuse play into the topic you are exploring.

Table 8.2. Examples of STEAM Board Games

Board Game	STEAM Connection	Skills and Concepts	Target Age
Robot Turtles	Coding	Programming logic, sequencing, debugging, functions	4+
Math Tac Toe	Math	Addition, subtraction, multiplication, mental math skills	8+
Suspend	Engineering, physics	Hand–eye coordination, cognitive skills, balance, counterbalance, cause and effect	8+
Planet	Environmental science	Problem-solving, strategic thinking, logical thinking, ecosystems, habitats	8+
Code Master Programming Logic Game	Coding	Programming logic, planning, sequential reasoning, and problem-solving skills	8+

DOLLPLAY

Dollplay is a type of pretend play that begins to develop in young children in their toddler years and in many children grows to be a favorite everyday play activity throughout preschool and early elementary. One survey, for example, of children between the ages of 4 and 12 found that over a third of children reported playing with dolls and toys as one of their favorite activities, but only when playing alone (Downey et al., 2007). According to Mattel, approximately 90% of American girls own at least one Barbie before age 11 (Griffin, 2009). Therefore, it is no surprise that many retailers have attempted to integrate STEAM content into the dollplay market. From ever-popular dolls like Barbie to smaller doll-focused start-ups, it is increasingly common to see dolls that reflect STEAM careers like astronauts, scientists, and more.

Surprise Powerz, for example, launched in 2021 with four talking dolls: Codie the Coder, Vera the Vet, Maria the Mathemagician, and Astro the Astronaut. These science-, technology-, engineering-, and mathe-centric dolls are designed to break barriers and encourage problem-solving while reflecting the diversity and potential of girls today, all while children are having fun. Each of these dolls has prerecorded words and phrases that encourage thinking and curiosity about the domain they focus on. Now, Surprise Powerz also offers classroom sets to promote STEAM dollplay in formal learning settings.

These dolls can be offered as part of other free play materials or used in conjunction with specific tools, curriculum, or products to teach or practice specific STEAM content. For example, astronaut dolls could be offered after a unit on astronomy. A coding-themed doll might code a robot alongside a young child (see Figure 8.1).

THE ROLE OF AN EDUCATOR IN EVERYDAY STEAM PLAY

What is the role of an educator when it comes to fostering child-led STEAM in everyday play? First and foremost, educators can make a plan to include play in everyday activities and explorations. This means considering logistics for providing the necessary time and space for regular child-led play. In planning, educators can build on what children already know and can do so that they can be successful in deepening their learning through child-led play that requires minimal adult intervention. Planning and organization may also involve reorganizing STEAM materials and toys to be easily accessible (e.g., physically at child level, in open bins) so that it is more welcoming for children and more likely to be discovered and played with.

In cases where educators may be playing alongside children, we recommend that they follow the children's lead. This means responding to their cues by joining in, imitating, and reacting to their actions. In cases where

Figure 8.1. A young girl playing with the Codie the Coder Doll and programming the KinderBot robot from Fisher-Price.

children are playing alone or with other young children, we recommend educators remember to OBSERVE, ASK, and PRAISE:

- **OBSERVE:** Children's play is a great time to make observations and learn what children are interested in, what skills they are working on, and the type of play they enjoy engaging with. This is a time to get ideas for topics that are personally meaningful and interesting to the students in your class so that you can, for example, build a full STEAM curriculum around their interests later on. Observations may also include taking pictures or videos to be used as part of assessments such as portfolios demonstrating work and skills mastered.
- **ASK:** Ask children questions to extend their play, deepen their learning, or scaffold a discovery they can make during their play.

Focus on asking open-ended questions that prompt deep thinking rather than having one simple "correct" answer. Additionally, "What if" questions can be used to stimulate curiosity and promote problem-solving skills that are relevant across all STEAM domains. These questions can be simpler than you may think. Some examples include:

  » What do you think might happen if you add another block here?
  » What is the story you are creating with these dolls?
  » Can you tell me how you built your structure so tall?
  » What if you wanted the bridge to hold more than one car? Would that be possible?

- **PRAISE:** When children engage in STEAM-based play and make a discovery, build a structure, learn to use a new tool, or engage in role-play as a scientist, doctor, or engineer, we can celebrate and further encourage their play by offering authentic praise. For praise to be authentic it should be specific and recognize not just a final *product* but the *process* children engaged with during their play. This may include praise like:

  » I noticed you rebuilt that bridge several times in order to make it hold the weight of three cars! I am so impressed that you didn't give up until you found a solution.
  » You have been working on this LEGO set for several days! It was a very complicated set with lots of pieces. I am so proud of you for completing it.
  » I love the colors you chose to paint your clay plate! You painted such a beautiful repeating pattern with the red and blue stripes.

CONCLUDING THOUGHTS

Integrating STEAM into everyday play provides young children with opportunities to explore, question, and create in ways that feel natural and engaging to them. By embedding STEAM elements into the toys, games, and activities children already love, we can nurture habits of mind like curiosity, persistence, and problem-solving while keeping the joy of play at the center. Everyday play offers interdisciplinary learning that is driven by children's imaginations and interests, ensuring that STEAM education remains accessible and meaningful. In the following chapters, we will look at more specific examples and settings for fostering STEAM play, including outdoors, in makerspaces, and through dramatic play and the arts.

CHAPTER 9

The Wonderful World of Outdoor STEAM

In this chapter, we focus on STEAM learning opportunities in outdoor environments. For most readers, the idea of outdoor play may conjure images of children playing in streams, balancing on logs, or otherwise exploring pristine landscapes, untouched by human tampering. However, we invite you to broaden this view and consider any kind of environment from the moment you step outside. A wonderful truth about exploring STEAM in the outdoors is that some of the most interesting learning can come from relatively commonplace, even urban, outdoor settings. Camping trips and nature walks are lovely for exploring natural phenomena, but as naturalist navigator and educator Tristan Gooley writes, "the ripples in a puddle will reveal things, just as the ripples in a pond and waves in the ocean will" (Gooley, 2016). In other words, water acts the same wherever it is, and there are amazing things to learn from any humble corner of the outdoors! The same could be said about wind, light, shadow, color, gravity, or any of the other fascinating science connections that are so readily available to experience once you step outside. But science is not the only STEAM discipline to explore in fresh air. Even human-made outdoor settings are fantastic sources for STEAM inquiry. Gaining a vantage of a tall building, a traffic light, a construction site, or the pattern of a brick wall can offer rich opportunities for wonder, observation, awe, and real-world relevance to practical questions of mathematics, technology, and engineering design.

Before focusing on how to build STEAM inquiry into an outdoor learning experience, it is worth pointing out the enormous physical, cognitive, and developmental benefits awaiting children when they spend more time outside. A systematic review of research on outdoor play including educational outdoor settings (Fermin et al., 2024) revealed the following influences on children's growth compared to predominantly indoor settings:

- **Physical development:** Increased physical activity and improved motor skills
- **Mental health:** Reduction in stress and anxiety, enhanced mood and well-being

- **Cognitive development:** Enhanced problem-solving skills, and improved creativity and imagination
- **Social development:** Increased cooperation and collaboration, improved communication skills with age-mates and adults
- **Sensory development:** Increased multisensory experiences engaging all senses (especially compared to sensory-limited experiences like watching screens); improved sensory integration and processing

These benefits are a main cause behind a growing movement of "nature preschools," "forest kindergartens," and other outdoor learning environments, specifically designed to support all-season outdoor play and nature education (Larimore, 2020; Sobel, 2016).

Relevant to STEAM education, outdoor settings also encourage curiosity and exploration, allowing children to foster the innate sense of wonder that characterizes many of the world's most prominent inventors and scientists (Correia et al., 2024; McClain & Vandermaas-Peeler, 2016). Natural settings encourage independent exploration and investigation, critical

Figures 9.1, 9.2, and 9.3. Images from a nature- integrated preschool: A child in a snowsuit drags a sled to a snowy hill (left); the school's outdoor equipment includes running water and a working firepit (center); pots and pans are hung from the playground fence to connect to the classroom's curricular theme of sound and music.

practices for authentic STEAM inquiry (Becker et al., 2017). Early nature experiences also support children in developing a sense of environmental awareness and stewardship, which manifests in STEAM learning as an urge to understand and safeguard natural resources and biological systems in the local and global environment (Chawla, 2009; Louv, 2008).

OUTDOOR PLAY AND STEAM

A team of researchers from Florida International University conducted a meta-study on the role of nature education programs on children's behavioral and academic learning outcomes (Fermin et al., 2024). The studies represented more than 1,200 child participants, ages 2–5, attending a variety of program types from nature programs to schools, set in mixed green landscapes including forests, playgrounds, farms, trail systems, schoolyards, gardens, and more. Interestingly, they found that across these diverse education programs, settings, and students, almost all of the studies characterized the activity of participants while outside in the same way: "child-led free play." This goes to show how intrinsically related outdoor time and play truly are, that they are used almost interchangeably in dozens of recent and prominent research studies. What is it about natural environments that seems to spontaneously spark child-led independent play, which can feel so elusive for children in an indoor classroom?

There are many possible answers, but one of our favorites comes from Nicholson's loose parts theory, which basically asserts that the typical indoor environment is prepared for a specific purpose and thus is closed to the creative possibilities of children (Nicholson, 1972). Nicholson argued that most cultural environments (including educational ones like schools and playgrounds) are "clean, static, and impossible to play around with," which can only be mended by incorporating what he called loose parts: unstructured materials that can be moved, connected, rebuilt, and generally tinkered with to create infinitely more possibilities for creative play than static materials. If you are having trouble envisioning a loose parts–rich environment, imagine a traditional children's classroom and consider the difference between a wooden block area and a writing desk. In your imagination, what do you see children doing in these two environments? If you thought of a child sitting calmly while writing or reading alone at the desk, versus a small group of classmates talking and building together on the floor at the block center, you have just demonstrated the simple power of loose parts to invite children into creative and open-ended play. Now consider the difference between a child's classroom and a forest floor or a garden. In contrast to the neatly stacked books, sorted toys, and the general symmetry and organization of the indoor environment, imagine the hundreds if not thousands of "parts" children can explore in a bed of leaves, a pile of sticks, or a gravel walkway. In the context of loose parts theory, it seems almost impossible for children *not* to play outside!

How does this all relate to STEAM education? In earlier chapters, we described how STEAM learning can happen most effectively through play that is curiosity-based, child-led, and authentic. Outdoor learning settings naturally support all three of these play approaches, leading to children who are primed and ready to learn STEAM concepts and practices. This might explain why so many formal science topics that confuse students in a classroom don't actually "stick" until children have some formative experience at camp or on vacation! As children naturally engage in curiosity-driven, self-led, and authentic play in outdoor settings, the availability of loose parts, open space, and free time supports easy, spontaneous involvement with many STEAM disciplinary topics and skills outlined in formal school curricula. Table 9.1 provides examples of specific concepts and practices within each STEAM discipline that are made highly concrete and visible in natural settings.

As you read through the STEAM practices in Table 9.1, you might wonder how to invite children to play in ways that leverage one or many of these activities during any given visit to the outdoors. Remember that the goal of STEAM play is not to be completely unstructured and unplanned, even if it might feel that way to the child. Just as with a playroom or classroom, you can still prepare an outdoor environment to support a specific kind of playful learning or investigation that you think your children might be ready for.

Table 9.1. STEAM Concepts and Practices Made Relevant in Outdoor Education

	Concepts	Practices
Science	1. *Environmental Systems*: Patterns of change in the local environment (e.g., weather, seasons, erosion and decay) 2. *Life Cycles*: Stages of growth in plants, insects, and animals 3. *Properties of Materials*: Behavior of materials like water, soil, and sand in different conditions (e.g., wet/dry, hot/cold) 4. *Ecosystems and Habitats*: Systems of living organisms that depend on each other in different environments (e.g., ponds, forests)	1. *Scientific Observation*: Using senses to explore and notice surroundings 2. *Classification*: Grouping plants, rocks, or insects based on characteristics (e.g., color, shape) 3. *Hypothesis Testing*: Predicting what will happen (e.g., to planted seeds) or observing changes over time 4. *Recording Data*: Drawing, writing, or narrating observations about weather, plant growth, or animal behavior

(*continued*)

Table 9.1. *(continued)*

	Concepts	Practices
Technology	1. *Simple Tools*: Understanding how basic tools like magnifying glasses, watering cans, or binoculars help extend abilities 2. *Material Properties*: Learning how tools interact with natural elements (e.g., using buckets to move sand or water) 3. *Mechanical Movements*: Basic understanding of wheels, pulleys, and ramps in outdoor play settings like sandboxes	1. *Choosing and Using Simple Tools*: Handling tools for exploration, such as digging in the dirt or observing insects 2. *Exploring Natural and Human-Made Materials*: Comparing the function and durability of items like sticks vs. plastic in building 3. *Designing and Experimenting With Simple Machines*: Building ramps, levers, or water channels with natural materials
Engineering	1. *Design and Structure*: Understanding how materials can be combined to create stable structures 2. *Problem-Solving*: Exploring how to use natural materials to solve challenges (e.g., building a shelter or a bridge) 3. *Force and Motion*: Learning basic ideas of push, pull, and gravity through play with objects	1. *Building Structures*: Designing and constructing with sticks, rocks, and leaves (e.g., creating shelters or bridges) 2. *Testing Designs*: Experimenting with water flow in small channels or testing which structures can stand up to wind or rain 3. *Iterative Design*: Modifying and improving structures based on trial and error (e.g., making stronger dams or bridges)
Arts	1. *Natural Patterns and Designs*: Recognizing patterns in nature (e.g., symmetry in leaves, spiral shells) 2. *Color and Texture*: Exploring different colors and textures in nature (e.g., tree bark, flowers) 3. *Creative Expression*: Understanding how materials from nature can be used for artistic creation	1. *Creating Art With Natural Materials*: Using leaves, sticks, stones, and other natural materials to create collages, sculptures, or mandalas 2. *Sketching and Drawing*: Observing and representing the environment through drawing or painting 3. *Music and Movement*: Using natural sounds (e.g., birds, wind) or materials (e.g., sticks, stones) to create rhythms or dances

(continued)

Table 9.1. (*continued*)

	Concepts	Practices
Mathematics	1. *Counting and Quantities*: Recognizing numbers and quantities in natural environments (e.g., counting leaves or petals) 2. *Shapes and Geometry*: Identifying shapes in nature (e.g., round stones, triangular leaves) 3. *Measurement*: Understanding length, volume, and weight through natural materials (e.g., comparing sizes of rocks or depth of water)	1. *Sorting and Categorizing*: Grouping natural objects by size, color, shape, or texture 2. *Measuring With Nonstandard Units*: Using sticks or footsteps to measure distances or the height of objects 3. *Pattern Recognition*: Creating or identifying patterns with leaves, stones, or flowers in outdoor settings

In the following sections, we consider ways to invite children at different age ranges into playful STEAM inquiry in outdoor settings. The natural world is the most perfectly differentiated environment for education that one can imagine, since humans evolved to attend to almost all aspects of natural settings in rich and unseen ways. Because of this, many natural settings and activities (e.g., nature walk, class garden) will work for the entire age 2–8-year range and beyond. However, the types of activities, conversations, and learning targets you look for will change to match narrow age bands (Wood, 1997).

OUTDOOR STEAM WITH TODDLERS (2–3 YEARS)

Naturalist and outdoor educator Tristan Gooley writes, "It should be expected that we will find wonder in a vast mountain landscape, but it is a more serious challenge to find wonder in a hill. It is a great achievement to find it in a molehill" (Gooley, 2014). Anyone who has spent any time with a toddler knows that they perform this great achievement many times a day, almost any time they are able to walk on a gravel or dirt path. At this stage, outdoor STEAM activities should emphasize exploration of textures, sounds, and sights, encouraging toddlers to touch, smell, and observe. Far from simple "time filling," sensory experiences like collecting leaves or rocks, splashing in puddles, or watching insects provide a critical foundation for STEAM habits of observation, inquiry, estimation, and expression. Conversations can focus on naming objects, discussing their material properties (e.g., soft, rough, wet), and observing basic patterns in nature,

Figures 9.4 and 9.5. A toddler on an outdoor nature walk pauses to investigate a flower (left) and explores an indoor nature-themed sensory bin (right).

like how water moves on different surfaces. If you find it challenging to spend significant time outside with your young learners, nature-themed sensory or open play can be a useful way to extend the learning indoors (see Figures 9.4 and 9.5).

At this age, learning targets should focus on developing sensory awareness, motor skills, and a budding curiosity about the natural world. Very little is needed to prepare the outside environment for this level of self-guided discovery, but you might think carefully about selecting the location and frequency of your outdoor visits. Repetition and routine are critical for very young children to be able to build mental models involving predictions, so visiting the same outdoor environment frequently at the same time of day will build a strong base to explore variation and change. Returning to the same environment at different times of day or night, in different types of weather, and over the course of a changing season are all wonderful ways to support children in authentic inquiry around patterns of change in natural systems.

You can support scientific observation by drawing children's attention to simple noticings about the natural world and taking their observations seriously as well. Many 2–3-year-olds love to identify their favorite common sights or natural phenomena whenever they see them outside (e.g., airplanes, pebbles, the moon). Support their innate curiosity by joining in on the fun and responding enthusiastically as often as you can. The greatest challenge with this age range is typically also the most impactful teaching move, which is to savor the slow pace of exploration. Allowing the full 10 minutes they may require to investigate a small rock is one of the best ways to invite authentic play for young children, and you might be surprised how infrequently you notice any boredom.

OUTDOOR STEAM WITH PRESCHOOLERS (4–5 YEARS)

Four-to-five-year-olds are more independent from adults in their thought and play, and are drawn in by stories, concrete experiences, and intuitive explanations. You might find that many of the same activities that entertain toddlers are still engaging but can be made more complex with imaginative play and story contexts to deepen curiosity. For instance, a "mud kitchen" allows children to mix soil, leaves, and water to create pretend dishes, which fosters early chemistry-like thinking and an understanding of concepts like mixing, transformation, and material properties.

Preschoolers are naturally curious, so incorporating structured observation techniques like "Notice/Wonder" walks, where you take turns making observations and posing inferences about what you see, can help them engage more deeply with their surroundings. These walks encourage children to notice details in nature and ask questions, leading to discussions about their observations. A child might wonder why certain leaves are different colors or how ants build their homes. From a curricular standpoint, children's authentic wonderings are a perfect launch into a deeper investigation that might involve STEAM inquiry practices. Children at this age are very concrete thinkers and enjoy identifying, sorting, and classifying objects. Activities like sorting and counting materials found on a playground, conducting a nature scavenger hunt, or asking questions involving simple observations and predictions (e.g., "What do you think would happen if we pour water on this rock?") playfully reinforce their developing understanding of categories, observable properties, and pattern recognition.

A potential challenge of outdoor STEAM education with this age group is managing their short attention spans and varying levels of engagement. While outdoor settings are rich with opportunities for exploration, simple bugs, weather changes, or noises can lead to derailing distractions. To strike a balance between structured inquiry and allowing space for spontaneous exploration, educators can start outdoor experiences with some level of freedom and flexibility, and limit "instruction" to short bursts of guided observation, such as calling excitedly for students to come and look at the amazing bird nest you found and then allowing them to lead their own conversation. Especially if outdoor learning time is new for your context, keep behavioral expectations realistic and perhaps even limited purely to

Figure 9.6. Kindergarteners plant vegetable seeds in a school garden they helped to design. They also planned ahead of time what to do with the harvest (donate to a local food pantry).

adhering to safety protocols. You can always continue the rich, meaningful conversations in a more familiar indoor space.

OUTDOOR STEAM WITH ELEMENTARY STUDENTS (6–8 YEARS)

By this age, children are becoming more capable of abstract thinking, problem-solving, and collaborative work, making outdoor STEAM education especially impactful. They are ready to take on more structured inquiry-based projects and find meaningful patterns and connections in open-ended outdoor explorations. You can focus prompts and guided activities on developing hypotheses, testing them, and reflecting on outcomes. For instance, a garden project might involve planning, planting, measuring plant growth, and recording changes over time, introducing concepts like ecosystems, plant biology, and measurement.

Design challenges with clear and specific outcomes, such as building bridges or shelters from natural materials, work well with this age, as children now have the fine motor skills and executive functioning skills to focus on completing a complex building task. Collaborative projects are also much more productive for these students, who are now familiar and skilled at collaborative play. Children may be ready to launch scientific investigations and data collection studies, and could be excited by opportunities to engage in basic citizen science, such as collecting data on temperature, rainfall, or animal sightings for online research projects (with the educator managing all actual data recording and digital sharing to avoid unnecessary screen time). These experiences provide opportunities to apply basic math and science skills to analyze patterns and practice research skills in a real-world context.

A challenge for this age group is ensuring that outdoor activities are challenging enough to keep children engaged but not so difficult that they become frustrated. Keep engagement high by offering plenty of opportunities for self-directed exploration while modeling ways to allow curiosity to evolve into rigorous data collection, hypothesis testing, and model-making. This is an example of persevering through hard fun from the Playful STEAM Learning Framework. Encouraging students to pursue complex questions about the natural world is an easy way to add academic challenge to playful outdoor experiences. Elementary students benefit from clear guidance and goals, so be intentional in your expectation that they do not need to know or

Figures 9.7 and 9.8. After learning about mathematical fractal patterns in science class (left), a 3rd- grader identifies fractal leaf veins in nature (right).

even explore all the answers to the questions they ask, but you are interested in seeing them generate great questions as part of their outdoor play.

CONCLUDING THOUGHTS

Outdoor settings provide myriad ways to integrate STEAM practices into authentic and playful inquiry about the natural world. Here are some of our favorite examples of STEAM-integrated learning experiences, organized from more foundational and appealing for younger children, to more advanced and likely to excite elementary-aged learners:

- **Water and Ice Play:** Set up a water table or a shallow bin with ice cubes. Let children explore how ice melts and how water feels, introducing basic concepts of temperature and states of matter through sensory play.
- **Leaf and Flower Sorting:** Collect leaves and flowers of different sizes, shapes, and colors. Encourage children to sort them by these characteristics, introducing basic classification, pattern recognition, and counting.
- **Barefoot Texture Walk:** Guide children on a barefoot walk on different outdoor surfaces like grass, sand, and smooth stones. Encourage them to describe or react to the different textures, engaging their senses and building vocabulary around touch and sensation.
- **Bubble Science:** Create a bubble station with various bubble wands, and let children experiment with making bubbles of different sizes and shapes. Discuss what makes bubbles float, pop, or stick together, introducing basic physics concepts like air, surface tension, and shapes.
- **Cairn Stacking/Rock Balancing:** Encourage children to stack rocks or natural materials, exploring balance, gravity, and basic engineering concepts as they experiment with different ways to make their structures stand.
- **Shadow Capture:** Using chalk, students can trace shadows of objects or each other at different times of the day to observe how shadows change with the sun's position. This activity incorporates math (measuring shadows), science (understanding sunlight and Earth's rotation), and art (creating shadow designs).
- **Leaf Printing with Cyanotype Paper:** Provide children with cyanotype paper and a variety of leaves. Allow them to arrange the leaves on the paper and expose it to sunlight, creating distinct silhouettes as the paper undergoes a photochemical reaction. Discuss how different leaf morphologies affect the final designs,

the science behind the cyanotype process, or identifying other photosensitive materials in nature (e.g., our skin when we get a sunburn).

- **Weather Station:** Have students build simple weather instruments like rain gauges, wind vanes, or barometers from household and natural materials, and/or provide store-bought versions of these tools. Collect data and make observations about changing weather and seasonal patterns.
- **Leaf Chromatography Art:** Have students collect leaves from different trees and use chromatography paper to separate the pigments in the leaves (especially interesting with autumn leaves). This introduces concepts of plant biology and chemistry as students observe the different pigments that make up leaf colors.
- **Fractal Walk:** Introduce a basic definition of a fractal pattern (a pattern that looks the same no matter how close or far you zoom in to look at it) and a few visual examples; then lead an outdoor hike to find fractals in nature (e.g., pine cones, ferns).

Facilitating outdoor education can feel like a carefully choreographed dance of balancing open play and drawing children back to the mindset of intellectual curiosity, but when done correctly, the experience for children is typically one of joyful play and freedom while exploring their own interests outside. Educators should remember to focus on avoiding the rush of finishing a task, getting a certain answer, or completing a worksheet in favor of letting children lose track of time while they become immersed in whatever direction sparks their curiosity. Even if their activity feels "off-topic" for your lesson plan, children may be communicating that they need to hone the practice of sustaining attention on ideas they are innately interested in before they can focus on the phenomenon you want to draw their attention to. Sometimes a gentle nudge is all it takes to redirect a child to a rich inquiry task, and other times you may find that granting them a bit of freedom reveals that they were thinking about or trying to access your intended task in a new way but engaging in self-led discovery while they did it.

CHAPTER 10

Makerspaces and Messy Play in Early Childhood

Makerspaces are community-driven environments where individuals come together to create, invent, and learn. These spaces have been pivotal in reshaping educational landscapes. They serve communities from young children all the way to professional designers and engineers, but what they all have in common is offering "makers" the tools and freedom to engage in hands-on, project-based exploration. Researchers argue that all makerspaces are also inherently educational, as they are sites where tools, techniques, and mentors are all concentrated primarily to help build knowledge and experience in novice makers (Honey & Kanter, 2013). As educational spaces, makerspaces fill a niche that may have been filled in past generations by woodshops, home economics classes, and automotive garages, but today they are synonymous with tech, engineering, real-world innovation, design thinking, iterative problem-solving, and deep mastery of complex skills (Hsu et al., 2017).

Learning that happens in makerspaces is often a beautiful example of the playful STEAM pillar of "persevering through hard fun," since most projects are self-motivated and engage students in much deeper and richer investigations than they might pursue if simply instructed to in a classroom. The predominant attitudes in makerspaces that encourage learner agency and exploration for its own sake create a safe space for educators to support student-led investigations, even when they are unlikely to result in functional or finished projects (Sheridan et al., 2014). In the next three sections of this chapter, we share illustrative examples (all based on true anecdotes) of lessons and projects in makerspaces for young children that both support interdisciplinary STEAM inquiry and forefront maker-led investigations and explorations.

PLAYFUL STEAM MAKING

Vignette: Cardboard Construction with Bernice (2.5 years)

Bernice is playing in her day care center makerspace with one of the cardboard boxes that her maker teacher, Ms. Dee, has brought in for the class to play with. Bernice's box is so big that she can fit all the way inside of it! She is having fun playing hide-and-seek from inside the box, but she keeps asking Ms. Dee for help closing the "door" (the top panel of the box) all the way. Ms. Dee finally asks Bernice if she wants her to add door handles to the box, and Bernice agrees.

Ms. Dee gets out a marker and draws a small rectangle near the edge of the top panel that Bernice has been using as a flapping door. Ms. Dee then draws a matching rectangle on the opposite panel, and she takes a pair of electric scissors out of her locked storage cabinet. Before she turns them on, she asks Bernice to put on safety goggles, keep her hands behind her back, and stand two big steps away from the box if she wants to watch. When Bernice is ready, Ms. Dee uses the scissors to cut over the lines that she drew, leaving two small openings in the panels.

Ms. Dee hands back the box and, it takes Bernice one or two more rounds of hide-and-seek to realize that she can now pull the box "doors" closed herself, by putting her fingers through the holes to push and pull. She tests this out a few times and then goes to the craft cupboard for a crayon. After a few minutes, she has drawn some lines on the box and brings it to Ms. Dee. "Window, please!" she asks excitedly, and waits for Ms. Dee to cut out exactly along the lines she has drawn. Some lines connect and leave small holes, and other lines are just slits in the cardboard. Bernice is delighted and shows her classmates. She asks Ms. Dee to take photos to share with her parents at home. For the next few weeks, whenever her class came to visit the makerspace, Bernice and several other friends drew cut lines on different materials—paper, cardstock, cardboard, and cloth—and asked Ms. Dee to cut them out. She plans to let the children continue this play for another 2 weeks before introducing a new play invitation, and in the meantime she wonders how she will wrap up this project and evaluate the students' learning.

In this story, Ms. Dee made a number of skilled educator choices that allowed Bernice to play with STEAM concepts. First, she knew how to let Bernice lead the play before stepping in as an expert maker. She waited to observe an experience Bernice was having and noticed a problem, namely, needing an adult to help her play the game she invented. In your own practice, if you're not sure when children are having a real problem, you can always look for moments when they are asking for a lot of help. For example, does a young child really need help to wash their hands, or can

Figure 10.1. Amanda Strawhacker helps a student decide on a cutline for their cardboard cutting project.

they just not reach the sink? Is there anything you can do to make it possible for them to do this safely and independently, so they don't need to ask for help so much?

Ms. Dee also knew when to model for Bernice how to plan and execute a design idea. Importantly, she first asked if Bernice *wanted* her to change the game by cutting her box. Children at this age have very little true control over their world, and as educators we want their creative play to be a safe place where they make the rules. Even if you have an idea that you know would be helpful and they would probably enjoy it, it's important to respect a toddler's decision to seek help or not. In this case, Bernice said yes, so Ms. Dee modeled how to draw a hole. If she had said no, Ms. Dee could have continued to observe and perhaps offer the same idea later or suggest a different play extension.

Ms. Dee made some subtle decisions about how to model the design process for Bernice. Drawing out her design plan (the lines on the cardboard) was an important step that she could have skipped. As an adult who is familiar with using scissors, she could very likely have created a functional hole without the cut lines. But then she would have missed out on an easy opportunity to show how adult makers and engineers *think* about a task before they *act*. She also offered an entry point to the activity that was familiar and accessible to Bernice. Using the electric scissors is not something that Bernice would or even should be allowed to do herself, but drawing a line where she wants an adult to make a cut is both empowering and accessible for a toddler.

Finally, Ms. Dee finished her plan and cut out a hole in the place where Bernice was missing a handhold. It is unlikely that at this age, Bernice would ever have thought to ask for that herself. It takes years of experience with the world to recognize that things can be changed and rebuilt, and it's possible Bernice had never even seen anyone change cardboard that way. By offering to cut a hole in the box *after* Bernice had started playing with it, Ms. Dee not only showed that cardboard can be manipulated like a building material, she also demonstrated very clearly *why* it might be useful to cut a hole in a box. Now it is much easier for Bernice to play her game! That is a very relevant and useful application for cardboard cutting that Bernice will remember for a long time. In fact, it was so impactful that even after she had finished playing with her hide-and-seek box, she continued to practice the play routine of (1) drawing cut lines in different materials, (2) asking Ms. Dee to cut them for her, and (3) examining the newly transformed materials.

Some teachers might be wondering what is the right amount of support to give to a student at this age. Is too much help "leading" them and stifling their creativity? While young children do need freedom and self-direction, they also benefit from occasionally observing a skilled and more experienced person (notice that we did not say "older"—children can learn a lot from watching each other, as well!). Instead of leading them away from their own creative path, think of your own STEAM play as opening a new pathway that they might never have known was available. In most cases, this is plenty of inspiration to give a child ideas of their own for weeks afterward. In the example above, Ms. Dee was able to join in Bernice's play and seamlessly hand off the creative power of drawing cut lines after just one example design. Bernice's own curiosity, rather than Ms. Dee's teaching, can now drive the educational work of testing, making predictions, and learning from her design experiments.

Now let's think of the Playful STEAM Framework and consider the pedagogy, strategies, and evaluation techniques that Ms. Dee used in her planning and teaching. In this case, her goal was to empower students to pursue their own maker projects and use tools independently, rooting her approach in authentic play. To do this, she used a very learner-centered approach of observing what activities children were curious about and providing opportunities to develop their skills further using specialized tools. Ms. Dee collected photos of Bernice drawing lines and watching the cuts being made, and kept one or two artifacts for Bernice to continue working on, which allowed a simple exploration to evolve into a longer-term project of cutting and designing with boxes. This addresses her pedagogy and strategies, but this story ended before Ms. Dee decided on her evaluation. If we review the PLAY pillars (Persevering through hard fun, Listening to children's ideas, Actively supporting inclusion, and saying Yes to open-ended sensory play), we can also see that she touched on perseverance and listening to children's ideas. If Ms. Dee wanted to go further with listening to children's ideas and supporting learner-centered play to focus on incorporating youth voice, what might she explore? Since she has yet to formally evaluate this experience, she might conduct a two- to three-question interview with Bernice to let her share more about what she loved and learned through her cutting inquiry. She could allow Bernice to narrate an imaginative story about her finished project that Ms. Dee could write down. She might also show Bernice the photos that she took throughout the project and ask Bernice to present them to her or to some classmates by describing what is happening in each photo. Any of these approaches would incorporate youth voice and also allow Ms. Dee to evaluate Bernice's experience and takeaways from the project. Alongside her observations of Bernice's changing design skills over time, the questions and comments Bernice made while working, and her finished artifacts, Ms. Dee could tell a persuasive and comprehensive story of Bernice's STEAM play and skill development over the course of a month of makerspace visits.

CHALLENGES IN THE PLAYFUL MAKERSPACE

In the previous example, we saw a neat and tidy example of how a makerspace facilitator can support playful STEAM learning. But what if you already run a makerspace and you aren't seeing the kind of natural, joyful, STEAM-infused play that we described in the rosy story above? It's very common for makerspaces (or any site of unstructured, child-led, messy play) to become less and less used for their intended playful purpose and for educators to feel a bit lost. In many cases, a makerspace can become just another room in a school, library, or home where traditional classroom-style learning takes place, without any of the emphasis on invention and creativity that a makerspace is designed to foster. If this sounds familiar, we encourage you to revisit the Playful STEAM Learning Framework and interrogate the ways that STEAM-based play infuses your activity.

Let's look at a different sample makerspace lesson. This story may or may not feel realistic to your setting, but either way please remember there is nothing inherently wrong with the following example as an approach to maker education. In fact, it may showcase an excellent way to foster some aspects of learning and exploration in young children. The point of this exercise is to reflect about how to adapt any activity to support playful STEAM learning. As you read, remember the PLAY acronym, and try to identify how these different elements are highlighted, which aspects (if any) are missing, and how you know.

Vignette: Building Bridges in Kindergarten STEM Class (5–6-year-olds)

The kindergarten students in Mrs. Clarke's elementary school have been participating in STEM class as a weekly "special" since the beginning of the school year. Mrs. Clarke is always coming up with crafty ways for them to explore new topics in engineering and technology. This month, she has introduced the theme of their work as "Building Bridges," specifically bridges that move to allow ships to pass under them through waterways. To help students understand how different bridge constructions work, Mrs. Clarke has already shown them videos of different moving bridges and explained how they function using counterweights and hydraulics. Today is the final day of the unit. Mrs. Clarke has built LEGO examples of three common moving bridges: a swing bridge, a bascule bridge, and a lift bridge. Students can play with the constructions she has made and build their own cityscape surrounding the bridges. They are also encouraged to test how the bridges move by pushing and pulling little levers that Mrs. Clarke has labeled with tape on each bridge model.

The kindergarteners have a fantastic time playing with the models and lifting and lowering the bridges. As their homeroom teacher, Mr. Brendan, comes to pick the students up from Mrs. Clarke's makerspace, he asks a small group to describe the LEGO bridges they are playing with. The three students playing at the bascule bridge model describe in detail about the ice cream shop and pet park they built next to the bridge. Mr. Brendan presses for more details specifically about the bridge mechanism. The students do not remember the name of it, but they can use their hands to show how it should move by opening up like a flower, then closing again. They ask Mr. Brendan if the school library has books on bridges that they could read at circle time.

What did you notice in this story? Did anything surprise you? Was anything missing that you might have expected? Let's use the STEAM activity features of pedagogy, strategies, and evaluation to describe the lesson, imagine the intended learning goals, and look for evidence of what learning the children took away (see Table 10.1).

What do you imagine Mrs. Clarke's learning goals were for the students? What might she be proud of as she reviews the highlights of this project? Student engagement and enjoyment was clearly high, and allowing 5-year-olds to manipulate working models of moving bridges provides some high-quality architecture exposure. Mrs. Clarke may have been aiming for students to practice observing and manipulating models in order to build theories about their function, which is a kindergarten-level learning standard (NGSS, 2013). If that was her goal, she may be especially proud that her students gained early experience with engineering mechanisms that most

Table 10.1. Pedagogical, Instructional, and Evaluation Strategies From Bridges STEAM Activity Example

Pedagogy	Instructional Strategies	Evaluation
Expert demonstration: Mrs. Clarke selected a theme (bridges) and provided highly authentic real-world examples of a specific category of bridge: moving bridges. She chose three common movement mechanisms (swing, bascule, and lift) to focus their investigations.	**Hands-on models:** She provided opportunities to observe moving bridges using a variety of media, such as video, verbal explanations, and interactive models.	**Enjoyment:** Students were on task and highly engaged throughout the class activity of building onto the bridge models. **Learning:** There was no obvious evaluative measure of content learning.

adults have likely never heard of and could not explain. From the perspective of exposure to professional-level engineering concepts, this project is a strong success. These outcomes speak to a very strong vision by the teacher of a phenomenon-based engineering activity that her students will likely remember for a long time.

Now put aside for a moment whatever opinions you might have about the effectiveness or educational opportunities of this activity, and consider its playfulness. Again, let's use the PLAY pillars to help clarify our observations:

- Persevering through hard fun: Students were invited to decorate and add onto working LEGO models of moving bridges. Based on their responses to direct questions about the activity, it appears the most engaging piece of the lesson for students was free-build with LEGO pieces to build an imaginative cityscape. While the project was fun for students, any challenge requiring perseverance seems to have been completed by Mrs. Clarke when she constructed the working bridge models ahead of time.
- Listening to students: Mrs. Clarke took the lead on selecting the bridges unit theme, building the models, and finding relevant research material. It is unclear from the story if she chose this theme based on evidence of student interest and aptitude, or her own idea of what would be manageable for her to teach, or from an external framework of learning standards (e.g., NGSS, 2013). There are opportunities to center the learner more in this process.
- Actively supporting inclusion: The project invitation supported them directly to explore and observe how bridge mechanisms function, and indirectly to imagine the civic context of a bridge and the communities who might use or live near it. The activity

seemed to draw on students' lived experiences of bridges so that all or most of them showed an entry point to participation. To invite more diverse ways of knowing about bridges, Mrs. Clarke might draw on historical and cross-cultural approaches to bridge building, such as sharing examples of movement bridges from countries around the world, discussing famous bridge engineers from diverse backgrounds, and showing photos of living root bridges cultivated by preindustrial societies.

- Yes to hands-on, sensory play: There are plenty of opportunities for hands-on play with LEGO bricks. Since the play is most directly tied to building the towns around the bridges rather than the bridges themselves, it makes sense that children are engaged in rich imaginative play around themes of towns and shops, with bridges serving as the backdrop for this neighborhoods and communities context. To forefront bridges as the learning topic of the play, an extension of the project might involve children playing and building bridges themselves, taking apart bridge constructions, or engaging in sensory play with things like materials that bridges are built from (small pieces of metal, bricks, etc.).

It would probably be fair to summarize the playfulness of the bridges activity by acknowledging that students were having a great time and engaging in lots of imaginative play, but perhaps not all related to the topic of bridges. From an educational perspective, it is difficult to know how successful this activity was in supporting rich learning about bridges. Students seemed to mainly take away the broad motions of the moving bridges, and experienced kindergarten teachers might question the developmental appropriateness of asking students to distinguish between the different machine systems introduced in the unit. Considering the time that Mrs. Clarke must have spent building the LEGO models during her planning period, one could argue that this lesson involves a heavy amount of teacher preparation for relatively low student learning payoff.

This story illustrates a challenge that many maker educators face, namely, how to engage their students in authentic play that still maintains the spirit of STEAM inquiry. Teachers can rely on their own inventiveness and expertise to create engaging and inspiring "museum-style" models and demonstrations, only to have students use them as props in their own games and play activities. Another common makerspace challenge is designing an activity that relies on a teacher's adult-level skill, creating a bottleneck when it comes time for students to move from designing to implementing. This type of issue is especially apparent in spaces with limited digital tools, where, for example, you might see a classroom of students who have finished designing their 3D-printer files and are now waiting for a whole class period or longer while their teacher has to edit and print off each piece one by one.

There is a happy medium between these very teacher-led, time-consuming lessons and starting from scratch with a new plan. Within the Playful STEAM Learning Framework, there is space for teacher-led inspiration to open the gateway to student-directed play. For example, playing with model bridges would be a perfect launch activity to then inspire deeper, child-led play around bridges, transportation, and simple machine systems. In addition to keeping the workload lighter for Mrs. Clarke, this transition also results in topics that are more age appropriate and accessible for kindergarteners, and connects to other topics in the general studies and social studies curricula that students may be exploring. A hint that this could be an excellent *start* to a project, rather than its culmination, is that it left students still curious about bridges and asking their teacher for resources like library books to investigate their questions.

"HARD FUN" THROUGH MAKING

In Chapter 5, we talked about hard fun and the importance of persistence, grit, and authentic motivation to bring STEAM play from "schooling" to learning. While reading this last story, consider the role of Youth Voice in directing the outcome of this STEAM activity.

Vignette: Art Bots in STEM Club (7–8-year-olds)

For 3 weeks, a group of 2nd- and 3rd-graders (aged 7 and 8 years old) have been meeting in their school's STEM club to work on an "art bot" project. They saw videos of AI robots making art and wanted to try to make their own creative, artist robots using markers, toy motors, and cups. They followed a guide for children chosen by their club teacher, Ms. Frankie, but the project was complicated. They learned how to strip wires, connect batteries, and use electrical tape. It wasn't easy, and there were many moments of frustration, with some students even shedding a few tears. "Why isn't this working?" sighed Maya, her brow furrowed in concentration. "Maybe your wires are connected backwards," suggested Jack, peering over her shoulder. But they kept trying, and with each attempt, they got better at building their robots.

Ms. Frankie was getting a little worried. They should have moved onto the next project weeks ago. Would the students feel so frustrated that they never tried circuitry again? Would the parents feel upset that they were stuck on the same project for so long? At the beginning of the 4th week, she offered the club a choice. They could choose to continue working on their robots, or they could bring home the unfinished work and move on to building something new. The students considered carefully, but everyone decided to keep working on their art bot.

Figure 10.2. Kindergarten students build and test "art-bots" to create an artistic mural.

Finally, they were ready to test the robots. Each child picked a marker color for their robot to draw with on a big canvas. "I'm choosing blue! What about you?" asked Emma. "I'm adding THREE colors!" replied Noah. The kids laid out a huge length of butcher paper and watched with excitement as their bots moved around, creating colorful patterns together (see Figure 10.2). When they finished, they decided to keep the artwork their robots had created, calling it a mural. "We did it!" cheered the group, proud of their hard work and teamwork. They asked Ms. Frankie if they could get permission to hang their mural in the school's maker lab for everyone to see.

This story showcases the buy-in that motivates students to work through challenging projects. No amount of forcing would entice students of any age to invest their learning and effort into a hard project like building a circuit, but by allowing the students to choose how to spend their time, Ms. Frankie quickly found that actually, most students enjoy a challenge when they are offered plenty of time and resources in a low-stakes environment.

CONCLUDING THOUGHTS

Makerspaces offer a dynamic platform for young children to engage in hands-on, interdisciplinary STEAM learning. (See Figure 10.3 for a project example.) By providing access to tools, guidance, and the freedom to explore, these spaces nurture curiosity, creativity, and resilience through real-world problem-solving and experimentation. Choose tools that foster collaboration and group play to allow ideas to flow naturally among makers.

Figure 10.3. Three 2nd- and 3rd-grade students work to hold together a "squishy circuit," composed of conductive Play-Doh and wiring, to light a series of colorful LEDs.

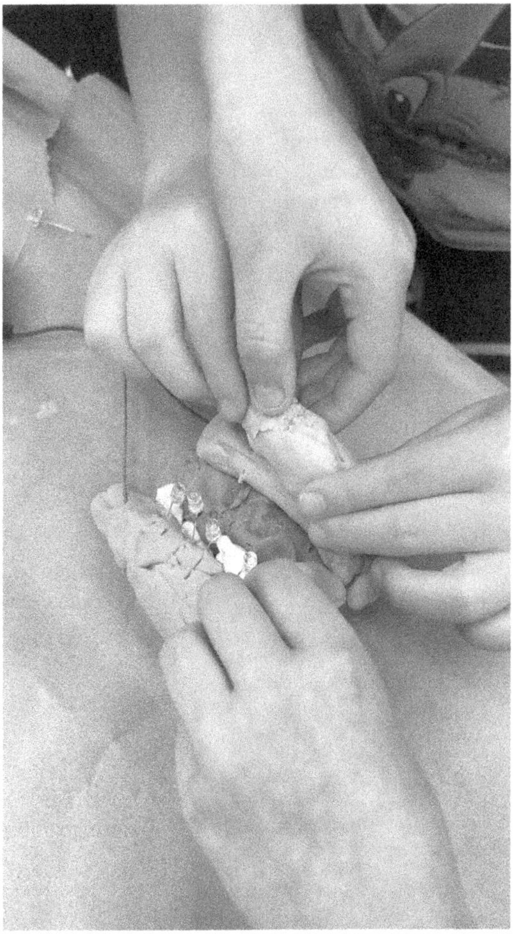

The open-ended, project-based nature of makerspaces not only fosters deep understanding across STEM and the arts but also promotes learner agency and perseverance. Table 10.2 highlights several of our favorite tools and practices for engaging children ages 2–8 in maker activities, organized from most foundational to most complex for this age range. As makerspaces continue to evolve, new and innovative tools and activities will continue to emerge to support makers at a variety of ages and developmental stages, but child-directed, authentic playful experiences will remain the key way to elevate these maker tasks to the level of STEAM inquiry investigations.

Table 10.2. Maker Tools and Practices for Children Ages 2–8

Age Range	Tools	Practices
Toddlers (2–3 years)	Cardboard and sturdy paper Cutout stamps Wax yarn sticks Oversized nuts and bolts Construction kit LEGO DUPLO Wooden building blocks Simple puzzles Play-Doh and clay Large beads and string for threading Magnetic building blocks Safe, chunky crayons and markers Pegboards with oversized pegs	Process art Material exploration Sensory play with textures Observing teachers using single tool for a specific job
Preschoolers (4–5 years)	Scissors Brads and hole punches LEGO Modeling clay and dough tools Foam building blocks Beads and lacing cords Simple sewing kits with plastic needles Painting supplies (brushes, watercolors, nontoxic paints) Construction paper and glue sticks Magnetic tiles Sand and water play tools (molds, scoops, sifters) Basic weaving looms Rubber band loom kits	Storytelling to immerse makers in creative tasks Experimenting with shapes, colors, and sizes of build materials Observing or using a small variety of simple tools to complete tasks Building simple structures

(*continued*)

Table 10.2. (*continued*)

Age Range	Tools	Practices
Early elementary learners (6–8 years)	Electric scissors/cardboard cutters Hot glue guns Hand drill LEGO Technic Simple circuit materials (batteries, wires and wire strippers, toy motors) Squishy Circuits, Snap Circuits Jr. and similar electronics kits Craft sticks and wood glue Basic sewing kits with real needles Small hammers and nails Kinetic sand Build-your-own-robot kits (age appropriate)	Collaborative problem-solving Designing and testing prototypes Making predictions Planning and executing multistep projects Comparing and selecting from a range tools for various prototyping or construction purposes

CHAPTER 11

STEAM and Dramatic Play

What exactly is dramatic play? Sometimes called pretend play, dramatic play is a type of imaginative play where children take on roles and act out scenarios. It's a form of symbolic play that may involve children using objects to represent other objects (e.g., a wooden block may represent a piece of chocolate cake), and can be real or imaginary. From playing "house" to playing dress-up, dramatic play is a major part of early childhood play and development.

Dramatic play is open-ended play and can involve a child playing alone or collaboratively with other children or adults. There are many benefits to dramatic play, including supporting creativity and self-expression. It can also help children learn and practice real-life skills and social skills. Dramatic play also gives children a safe space to explore and process issues, ideas, and fears that they come across in their lives. As such, many early learning settings include dramatic play areas with access to costumes and imaginary play setups (e.g., a pretend kitchen or pretend doctor's office).

By preschool, children have reached a peak period of pretend play (Singer & Singer, 1990), and up to two-thirds of the time they spend in pretend play is interactive (i.e., sociodramatic play with other children) (Rubin, 1986; Rubin et al., 1983). This type of pretend play may begin to gradually lessen in middle childhood as children become more interested in organized games and sports, but some reports indicate that older children may still engage in pretend or fantasy play, most likely privately (rather than with peers).

Dramatic and pretend play may also be an avenue for exploring STEAM skills, interests, and identities. A small but growing body of work supports the idea that imaginative play can support learning of the sciences. For example, Fleer (2009) points out that the link between imagination in science education and imagination in play is not utilized to the extent that it should be. An imaginary situation can support children's developing understanding of scientific concepts and processes, or it may even prompt children to produce talk that fosters their problem-solving (Caiman & Lundegård, 2018; Hakkarainen, 2008).

More recent research investigating how imagination and play manifest in young children's science inquiry (i.e., *scientific play*) conducted in Finnish preschool groups showed that scientific play emerges throughout inquiry and has four characteristics: creating and maintaining an imaginary science situation, assigning new meanings to science objects and processes, combining imaginary situations and realistic problem-solving, and engaging in science talk in an imaginary situation (Vartiainen & Kumpulainen, 2020).

STEAM DRAMATIC PLAY CENTERS

Given the importance of dramatic play in young children's learning and development, it is a rich area to support playful STEAM learning. In fact, through observations you may realize there is already a lot of STEAM learning happening in the dramatic play scenarios your young learners are engaging in. Some examples educators and caregivers have probably seen include:

- Practicing counting and money when pretending to shop at a store or supermarket
- Exploring careers like doctors and veterinarians when engaging in dress-up play and dramatic play with dolls and stuffed animals
- Pretending to use computers or invent robots as part of an imaginary storyline

Educators can further encourage dramatic play around particular STEAM themes and careers by setting up and offering dramatic play centers. A dramatic play center is a space where children can engage in imaginative play and explore different roles and situations. These centers are often found in preschool and kindergarten classrooms, as well as day cares, children's museums, and in at-home playrooms. Table 11.1 provides examples of some of the dramatic play centers you could consider setting up to encourage imaginary STEAM learning and play, such as shown in Figures 11.1–3.

Table 11.1. STEAM Dramatic Play Center Ideas

Center	STEAM Connections	Props to Offer
Farmer's Market	Food, farming, plants, vegetables, counting, money/finance	Baskets filled with items like pretend fruit, vegetables, eggs, and flowers; pretend cash register; play money; a working scale
Garden Shop	Plants, flowers, plant life cycles	Baskets, vases, and buckets filled with different kinds of pretend flowers, a pretend cash register, play money

(continued)

Table 11.1. (*continued*)

Center	STEAM Connections	Props to Offer
Supermarket	Food, fruits, vegetables, counting, money/finance	Different kinds of play food, a play shopping cart or basket, a pretend cash register, a supermarket employee apron/uniform, play money
Restaurant	Food, counting, money/finance	A table and chairs, play food, menus, play money, play cash register
Doctor's Office	Medical careers, health care	Doctor lab coats, pretend medicine, pretend first aid kits, pretend exam tools (e.g., stethoscope)
Veterinarian's Clinic	Veterinary careers, animals	Veterinarian lab coat, pretend medicine, pretend exam tools (e.g., stethoscope), realistic stuffed animals, play food for animals
Outer Space	Space-related careers, planets, astronomy	Astronaut costumes, rocket/spaceship pop-up tent, glow-in-the-dark stars, play telescopes, star maps
Under the Sea	Marine science, marine animals	Blue fabric to represent water, ocean animals, play fishing poles, play boat and life preserver, nautical flags
Scientist's Laboratory	Science-related careers, science tools	Science lab coats, beakers, pipettes, microscope, resin-encased insect or rock specimens, protective goggles
Computer Scientist's Office	Computer science–related careers	Child-size tables and chairs with pretend laptops and other pretend technology, notebooks with graph paper and writing instruments

Figure 11.1. Kindergarten children wear protective gloves and dramatic-play lab coats before working at a chemistry center.

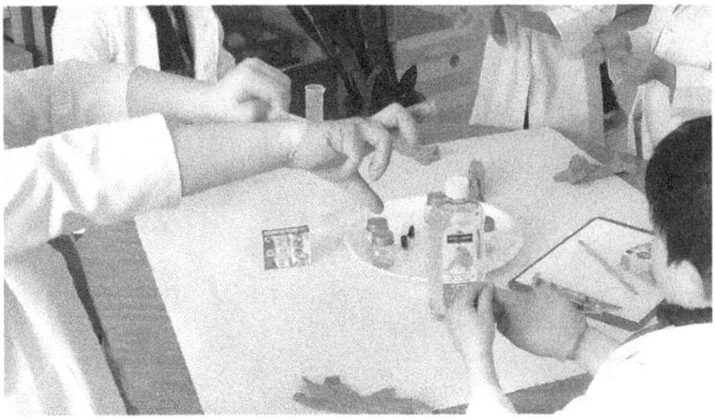

Figure 11.2. A kindergarten child dresses up as an astronaut in a space-themed dramatic play center.

Figure 11.3. A preschool child gives a baby a checkup in a doctor's office-themed dramatic play center.

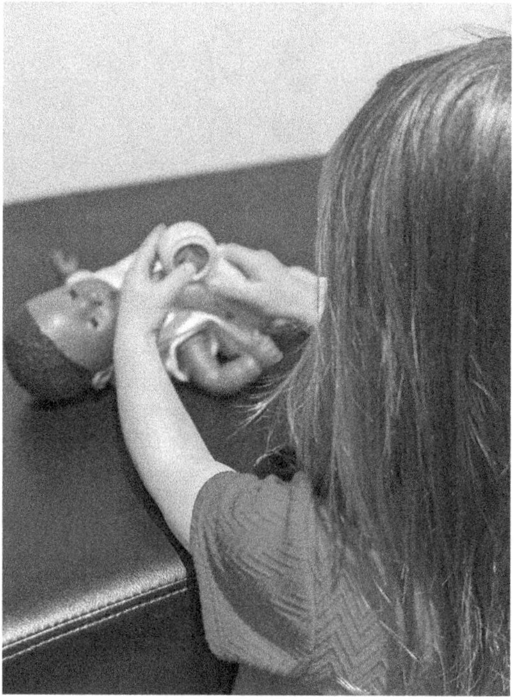

CULTURALLY RELEVANT DRAMATIC PLAY

When looking through the ideas presented in Table 11.1 and moving on to choose ideas for your dramatic play centers, it is important to consider whether the centers you are setting up will prompt authentic play that is personally and culturally relevant to the young children you work with. Culturally relevant dramatic play centers allow young children to engage in pretend play that stems from their lived experiences, as well as introducing novel scenarios they may have encountered in books and media. Props, materials, costumes, and toys allow children to reenact activities and observations that are relevant to their own family life and share common events in their cultures. Through this authentic dramatic play comes children's meaningful learning (Salinas-Gonzalez et al., 2018).

To ensure that the dramatic play setups you are offering your learners are culturally and personally relevant, educators should take time to regularly assess the materials and props in the dramatic play center to make sure they accurately reflect all of the children and families who might use the space.

Especially for public and broad-audience spaces, ensure that your play environment can also accommodate children with different backgrounds, neurodivergences, sensory needs, and disabilities (Salinas-Gonzalez et al., 2018). As a starting point, consider setting up a play area with accessible pathways (adding ramps if needed), including play materials and equipment at a variety of heights to accommodate diverse mobility levels, incorporating sensory experiences for children with different sensory needs, and more. Each public space will have different unique needs, and it is important to provide ongoing opportunities for soliciting and incorporating feedback from the community to cater to diverse needs of all learners who may use the space.

DRAMATIC PLAY AND THE DRAMATIC ARTS

The type of dramatic play we have described so far in this chapter is a form of play that can grow to become the foundation of drama more broadly. As children move through elementary school, the dramatic arts can build on the skills children develop through dramatic play. Their experiences with such play can lead to an appreciation or even a passion for the dramatic arts.

There are many ways to foster elements of dramatic arts education into the playful STEAM, such as including an oral storytelling or performative element to a science or technology exploration, integrating music or dance as a means to learn new STEAM skills, and using skits and improv to process and share new ideas. Let's explore a couple of examples before going into ideas and strategies you may wish to implement:

Attack Theatre: Teaching Science Through Theatre. Attack Theatre, a dance and interdisciplinary arts theatre in Pittsburgh, partnered with the science teachers at Pittsburgh Public School's Sunnyside Elementary School to create kinesthetic exercises that support the science curriculum for 3rd- and 5th-grade students.

> When science is presented through theatre, students aren't as afraid of getting things wrong and feel free to shout out, or even dance, answers. By integrating the safe and friendly space that is the theatre with the scary science world, we can help make bounds and leaps in trying to diversify the science, technology, engineering, and math (STEM) fields, helping the general public stay educated and up to date on science research.
>
> —Lina Pulgarin-Duque, dramaturge, physicist, and innovator

Dances From Around the World: Robotics + Dance + Performance. Through the Dances From Around the World robotics curriculum, developed by the DevTech Research Group, children in K–2nd grade learn foundational coding and robotics concepts while exploring concepts of music and dance. The curriculum culminates with children choosing a style of dance or music to research

Figure 11. 4. Amanda Sullivan, Amanda Strawhacker, and a colleague using puppet versions of the KIBO robot alongside actual KIBO robots to perform a short skit teaching coding and engineering concepts at Boston Children's Hospital.

and learn about, many of them choosing dances rooted in their own cultural heritage. They build and decorate their robot to represent the dance, and program their KIBO robot to perform their dance. Students learn their dance and have a robot + student performance recital as part of their final projects.

There are also many simple ways that you can choose to integrate a little bit of performance and the dramatic arts into your STEAM curriculum:

- **Skits:** Have students showcase what they have learned about a new concept through a skit they perform for the class.
- **Songwriting:** Create fun, rhyming songs that your class learns to help them master new facts and knowledge. These can be performed during showcases or open houses displaying students' work.
- **Puppetry:** Use puppets to help explain and explore complex topics in fun and engaging ways (see Figure 11.4).
- **Showcases/Performances:** Offer children many opportunities to practice public speaking and performance skills through showcases of their work. Be sure to rehearse many times to set them up for success in gaining recognition from their peers, family, and friends!

- **Watch performances:** Find performances that overlap with a concept or topic you are exploring in local children's theaters or community theaters to explore with your students.

CONCLUDING THOUGHTS

Dramatic and imaginative play helps children to make sense of the world around them, which is what scientific inquiry and foundational STEAM skills are all about. Early childhood educators can integrate STEAM into dramatic play in easy ways, from adding a few meaningful props to a dress-up area (e.g., adding lab coats, beakers, goggles, and other science costume props) to creating content-specific dramatic play centers (e.g., creating a farmer's market dramatic play center that allows children to explore their curiosity about food and farming). Educators can further integrate the dramatic arts by including storytelling, puppets, and other performance elements to their STEAM curriculum and activity planning.

Part IV

SCREEN-FREE TECHNOLOGIES FOR LEARNING

CHAPTER 12

Technology All Around Us

One of the most amazing things about how children learn is the way they seem to literally soak up information like sponges, repeating phrases and behaviors that they see around them as early as toddlerhood. In today's technology-rich world, it's no surprise that children very quickly understand that phones, computers, and televisions are fascinating sources of exploration. Even with low- or no-screen practices at home, no device time at schools, and plenty of outdoor and sensory play to offset or replace screen use, children seem to have a sixth sense in the form of an innate curiosity about technology. Our job as educators is not to stamp out the seeds of their interest but to water those seeds with the appropriate mix of supports to cultivate a healthy, responsible, and intellectual curiosity about the human-made and digital tools that children will encounter in their everyday lives.

NAVIGATING A TECH-RICH WORLD

Vignette: A Sensor Walk with Sonya's Class (Prekindergarten)

Sonya and her hallway buddy are holding hands and walking in a line with their classmates. They are walking a very familiar hallway in school that they use every day, but their science teacher, Mrs. Allard, has told them they will see this hallway with brand-new eyes. Mrs. Allard holds up her hands and sings the "Stop, Look, and Listen" song, and Sonya and her partner stop walking. "Does everyone remember when we explored the digital camera in class yesterday? Can I see one quiet hand from a friend who can remind me about the special part of a camera that helps it to see?" Noah raises his hand and remembers the word "lens."

"Very good! I see many friends showing me with their hands that they agree." Sonya thinks back to yesterday, when the class talked about the five senses that help humans see and hear things in the world. Mrs. Allard had said that machines and technologies sometimes have parts called "sensors" that help them take in information about the world, almost like humans can. Mrs. Allard continued, "The camera lens has a sensor inside of it. I want everyone to look with noticing eyes and quiet voices and give me a thumbs-up if you see something else that might have a sensor in this hallway."

The students look around for a while, and then Sonya sees it—a huge camera lens in the doorway of the school library! She whispers to her buddy and begins to jump excitedly up and down, thrusting her hand up high. "Sonya, you look like you've made a discovery! What do you see?" Sonya points at the lens high on the ceiling, and Mrs. Allard grins. "Exactly right! Security cameras also have sensors. Anyone else?" Navien raises her hand and points to the automatic door that opens when you walk close to it. "Ah, very good noticing, Navien! Yes, any door that opens automatically when you get close to it probably has a sensor somewhere inside to look for your body. If we look closely, can we see a sensor in this door frame?" Eventually, the students all see it and excitedly point out the location to their friends. Mrs. Allard lets children share a few more noticings before they continue down the hallway to their next stop at the service elevator.

Young children experience technology every day, perhaps without us even realizing it. Digital and "smart" technologies are pervasive in children's lives, from sensor-activated doors and faucets to robotic vacuum cleaners and voice-interactive speakers. Even analogue human-made tools such as wall clocks, record players, or radios can seem like magic to young children. As with print awareness and numeracy, children can benefit from naming and identifying these objects in their world long before they can understand how they work. By engaging them early in recognizing and interacting with technology, we can build foundational knowledge that fosters their natural curiosity while also instilling responsible and ethical habits of technology use. In the sections below, we'll explore practical strategies to help children navigate and make sense of the technology all around them.

TELL STORIES ABOUT TECHNOLOGY

One of the best ways to begin conversations about technology (or any STEAM topic that is unfamiliar to children) is to read books about technology themes and talk about technological objects and characters (e.g., robots) as you encounter them in the text. By inviting children to engage in storytelling and dramatic play with technology, you can open the door to talking about tools that might feel magical or even forbidden to children, depending on how screen time is handled at home and school.

Use stories to help children talk about technologies in everyday life, showing how they can help us solve problems or think in creative ways. You can build narratives that center on familiar objects, such as how a computer helps people communicate or how a robot vacuum cleans a house, or you can wonder together about wild examples of robots in space or exploring the deep sea. Talking about how humans use technology to help us with tasks or complete everyday jobs like cleaning makes technology more relatable, but more importantly, it introduces the idea that anyone—even children—can be creators and problem-solvers using technology.

NOTICE ENVIRONMENTAL TECHNOLOGY

Try this activity: Play a game with your children where you notice technologies around the room and ask them what they do. You might be surprised how many young children don't know how to explain the purpose of a remote control, computer, or a digital clock. Although these are technologies that we as adults interact with every day, children typically don't get officially introduced to the names, functions, and purpose of digital tools in their everyday environment. Point out technological tools around the house and in your community—like microwaves, digital clocks, radios, barcode scanners, computers, and phones—and invite children to ask questions about what these tools do and how they work. This simple activity helps demystify everyday technology, fostering curiosity and building foundational knowledge about the tools that shape our world.

PLAY WITH AND POINT OUT PARTS OF TECHNOLOGIES

Long before children can understand how screens or keyboards work, they are drawn to buttons, switches, and dials that control them. You can explore these when it is safe to do so or simply name and identify the different parts of technology tools to clarify their functions. As with a Montessori-style "busy board," which helps young children to build fine motor skills, grip strength, and mastery of locks and buckles, you can offer simple toys or powered-off tools to safely practice tapping, twisting, and flipping digital parts commonly found on technological tools. When children are playing with toys that have electronic features, which can feel particularly "magical" to them since they are often designed to look like normal stuffed toys or books, you can draw children's attention to parts like lights, battery packs, and on/off switches that give clues to their technological components. This can also build a foundational awareness for children to explore more complex ideas of technological components and engineering concepts, such as inputs, outputs, ports, and control switches.

ENCOURAGE SAFE TINKERING WITH TECHNOLOGY

Provide children with safe tools and technology, and encourage them to take devices apart and see if they can figure out how they work. Depending on children's fine motor skills, simple mechanized toys and household objects (like mechanical pencils) are great places to start! Some objects, like bicycles, don't even need to be fully disassembled to watch and learn how the mechanics in the system interact. Encourage children to ask questions as they tinker, prompting them to think critically about each part and its function within the system. Offer guidance on using simple tools like screwdrivers or pliers, always ensuring safety by supervising closely and providing *functional* child-size safety gear. Allowing children to explore freely within these boundaries fosters curiosity and problem-solving skills, confidence, and a sense of agency with human-made objects.

DO be mindful of serious hazards when initiating a technology take-apart project. In general, older TVs and any kind of batteries or power supplies should be avoided. The following objects are dangerous and should be avoided or removed before young children play:

- **Lithium batteries**, which are common in newer laptop computers, can combust and release toxic gases.
- **Tiny parts** like screws, bolts, and buttons are choking hazards for toddlers.
- **Coin-cell batteries** are extremely dangerous if ingested, posing severe risks such as chemical burns or choking.
- **Capacitors and power supplies**, especially from older electronics, can hold high-voltage charges even after the device is powered off and can cause electrical shock.
- **Sharp components**, such as broken glass from screens or jagged metal edges, can cause cuts or injuries.
- **Heavy objects**, like old monitors or TVs, can be physically dangerous if dropped or mishandled.
- **CRT monitors** (older televisions and computer screens) contain high-voltage tubes and hazardous materials like lead.
- **Power cords and electrical plugs**, especially if the wires are frayed or damaged, may expose children to the risk of electrocution.

LABEL TECHNOLOGIES

Use written words, pictures, and spoken names to label technologies around familiar learning and living spaces. When parts are labeled with names and icons, children can build a vocabulary of technology, making it less mysterious and more approachable. You can also use labels to explain the functions of technology parts and draw connections to similar parts around the world. For example, a radio might have a spinning knob to control the volume of its sound, while a TV remote might use buttons with up and down arrows to do the same thing. Notice similarities and differences in unfamiliar technological parts, such as the different keypads on a microwave and a phone, and draw students' attention to familiar aspects, like the numbers that look just like the ones in their favorite counting picture books. This kind of conversation and intentional "noticing and wondering" strengthens their understanding of individual devices and also helps them see the broader connections between various forms of digital objects in their local environment.

FOSTER INTELLECTUAL CURIOSITY WITH "HOW" AND "WHY" QUESTIONS

It may be easier to try avoiding technology entirely, but it can be productive to praise children's efforts to figure out *how* technologies work and what they are used for. Ask open-ended questions about tools, how they were made, who might use them, and what they might be for. Model your own curiosity by voicing aloud when you wonder how a technology works, and treat children's questions with serious reflection. Get in on the fun when children make up silly stories about a technology they've never seen before. What can their play tell you about their *real* questions, confusions, and wonderings? This creative exploration often reveals deeper questions that can lead to insightful conversations about technology.

HELP CHILDREN UNDERSTAND THE DIFFERENCE BETWEEN NATURAL AND HUMAN-MADE OBJECTS

The most important aspect of new technologies for young children to understand is that these tools were made by humans and are not natural. Encourage them to notice natural things in their day-to-day life: plants, animals, seasons. Tap into your inner science teacher to draw their attention to cycles of growth and change in living creatures, and their requirements for shelter or specific habitats, food and water, sunlight, air, and family.

Technologies do not grow, and they were not born or created by natural processes. In other words, they are not alive and never were. Children may notice that even technologies must have been made by natural materials, but they can usually also observe that digital tools are not natural themselves. What's amazing about digital technologies is that they are basically tools, just like a hammer, even if they are vastly more complex and carefully designed. You can play a game with children in which they look around a classroom or house and try to notice all the things that a human (specifically, an engineer) must have built. Eventually, children will realize that almost everything in most indoor environments is human-made! Technologies like computers and phones are no different. This means that just like when someone originally made them, someone else can change and improve them.

CONCLUDING THOUGHTS

Children love to imagine a future when they are older and more experienced at building things, and dream about all the technologies they will invent. By following these simple strategies for inviting them into the technological world from a young age, you can build their confidence and agency around STEAM topics, and set them on a path of lifelong technological tinkering and curiosity. While the technology they encounter may change and will likely be obsolete by the time they are grown, the creativity, resilience, inquisitiveness, and problem-solving skills that they develop through hands-on exploration will stay with them into adulthood. Empowering children to understand and use devices as tools eventually encourages them to express their ideas, innovate, and potentially contribute their own improvements to the technologies of their increasingly complex, data-driven world.

CHAPTER 13

Unplugged Computer Science for Hands-On Learning

In Chapter 3, we introduced the idea of computational thinking (CT) without computers. We introduced the perspective that young children can effectively develop CT skills like decomposition and sequencing without the need for computers, using unplugged activities or through role-playing, storytelling, and more. We presented evidence from studies suggesting that unplugged CT interventions are both successful and developmentally appropriate for early childhood and elementary schooling.

Now, you might be wondering, how *exactly* can you learn about computer science without a computer. In this chapter, we will dive deeper into the Computer Science (CS) Unplugged movement and a growing number of tools, games, and books that allow for playful learning and skill building in this area.

CS UNPLUGGED

The term *CS Unplugged* originated with a collection of activities that were shared online in the early 1990s in various formats, culminating in 1999 with a free online book coauthored by Tim Bell, Mike Fellows and Ian Witten called *Computer Science Unplugged: Off-Line Activities and Games for All Ages* (Bell et al., 1999). Since then, the material has been developed into lesson plans, activities, ideas for exploring CS Unplugged at home, and more much more, all available on the website www.csunplugged.org.

CS Unplugged has become a particularly powerful movement in recent years, in part because it allows people with little to no technical background to explore concepts that drive the technologies we use each day. In this way, the movement served as an outreach tool to engage the wider public—including those with no technical background and perhaps even apprehension about teaching with technology—with powerful ideas behind computer science and computational thinking. Additionally, it allows young children to explore concepts related to coding and CT without reliance on screen-based technologies. This makes unplugged computer science activities particularly appealing to those who work in early childhood education and hope to expose children to coding while still limiting screen time. Lastly, it promotes hands-on learning that is easily integrated across STEAM disciplines.

With the unplugged approach, you can think of computer science as a set of ideas that can be introduced even without actually coding. Unplugged activities place emphasis on promoting computational thinking (and all the associated skills described in Chapter 3), rather than focusing on learning the syntax of a particular coding language.

There are a wealth of resources available for unplugged activities on the CS Unplugged website that provide curriculum and activities for children ranging approximately from 5 to 14 years that involve cards, puzzles, crayons, string, and more. Examples of unplugged computer science activities include creating bead necklaces in binary with beads that represent 1s and 0s or using a grid and symbols to put classic fairy tales in a logical order. When it comes to interdisciplinary STEAM learning, the CS Unplugged website offers many activities and lessons that integrate with areas like literacy, mathematics, and even the performing arts, music, and biology. These activities were traditionally designed to be used with school classes and larger groups, but the website now offers a section on CS Unplugged at Home, which features activities that can be implemented in home settings or other informal, small group, or individual learning settings.

With the growth of the original CS Unplugged movement, many others have developed activities, curricula, games, and even digital technologies to explore coding concepts in screen-free ways. In the following sections, we will explore board games, card games, and screen-free programmable robotics kits for use in the early childhood years.

BOARD GAMES

There are a growing number of unplugged games and products being sold commercially to teach coding skills and concepts. For example, the Robot Turtles board game teaches coding concepts to children ages 3 and up (see Figure 13.1). Robot Turtles was created by software engineer Dan Shapiro, inspired by his own 4-year-old twins, and was the most funder-backed board game in Kickstarter history when launched. Playing the game is easy: You create a maze on the board with the turtles in the corners and the jewels in the center. Kids play instruction cards (such as turn right, turn left, move forward, etc.) in order to "program" their turtles to get to their jewels. The board can be set up differently each time, and as children get more familiar with the cards, more complex instructions can be used.

Since Robot Turtles was released, many additional board and card games have been created (see Table 13.1). These can be implemented in formal, informal, and home settings either to explore new concepts and

Figure 13.1. Robot Turtles board game.

Table 13.1. Examples of Coding Board Games for Young Children

Board Game	Age Range	Description
Robot Turtles	3+	Multiplayer board game with the goal of programming your turtle to navigate a maze to reach its jewel
LittleCodr	4+	A card game where kids get to program their parents or friends to do crazy things by using simple action cards
CoderMarz	6+	A board game that teaches Mars facts, coding, and artificial intelligence concepts using fun gameplay
Coding Farmers	7+	A game played with action cards in two ways, regular English and Java code; teaches kids to connect their actions with written code
Coding Master	8+	An avatar chosen by the child travels to an exotic world in search of power crystals; along the way teaching the children programming logic to navigate the map

terminology or to help reinforce concepts and ideas that have already been introduced through a formal lesson. As discussed earlier in the book, board games provide a wonderful opportunity to foster play (especially with older children) and to strengthen skills like turn taking, listening, respect, and being a "good" loser and winner on top of the coding concepts being taught.

SCREEN-FREE PROGRAMMABLE ROBOTS

While many children's programmable robots require the use of a tablet, phone, or computer to code, there are a growing number of screen-free robots designed for young children. Decades of work has shown that beginning in preschool, children can successfully engage with robotics. In research trials with simple robotics and programming languages, children as young as 4 years old demonstrated an understanding of foundational engineering and robotics content such as what a robot is, what robotic parts make robots move, and how to give a robot simple instructions (i.e., code) to make it move (Bers et al., 2002; Cejka et al., 2006; Perlman, 1976; Sullivan & Bers, 2015; Sullivan et al., 2013; Wyeth, 2008). In addition to them mastering this new content, programming interventions have been shown to have positive benefits for children's developing numeracy, literacy, and visual memory, and can even prompt collaboration and teamwork (Clements, 1999; Lee et al., 2013).

New developmentally appropriate technological software and robotic kits have evolved in the tradition of educational manipulatives like Montessori materials and Nicholson's loose parts, and like their predecessors, these tools allow children to explore their understanding of shape and number, spatial relations, and proportion (Brosterman, 1997; Kuh, 2014; Nicholson, 1972; Resnick et al., 1998). Robotics curricula are now also being developed to address children's need to move, dance, and push their physical boundaries. For example, when constructing a robot with many parts, children may exercise fine motor skills, and when observing a robot's movements, they are compelled to move and dance along, developing their hand–eye coordination and gross-motor activity (Resnick et al., 1998).

EXAMPLE: KIBO ROBOTICS KIT

KIBO is a robotics kit designed specifically to playfully introduce young children (pre-K through elementary school) to foundational engineering and programming concepts through unplugged play and activities. We, the authors of this book, both spent many years working on the conceptualization and development of KIBO, which was created based on research conducted by the Developmental Technologies Research Group at Tufts University

Table 13.2. Screen-Free Robots for Young Children

Robot	Target Age or Grade	How It Works
Bee-Bot	3+	Bee-Bot, a friendly bumblebee-inspired robot with arrows on its back, can be coded to move in any straight direction (forward, backward, left, or right) and can be used with visual coding cards to plan and keep track of which buttons are pushed in which order.
Code-a-Pillar	3+	This robot caterpillar comes to life when it is assembled using its interchangeable segment pieces. Each segment represents a different action, sending the caterpillar in a different direction every time.
Code 'n Go Mouse	4+	Children can create a step-by-step path for the programmable robot mouse. The mouse lights up, makes sounds, and features two speeds along with colorful buttons to match coding cards for easy programming and sequencing.
indi (by Sphero)	4+	With indi's onboard color sensor, children can communicate instructions to indi by placing color tiles on the floor that tell it what to do and where to go (and how fast!).
Kinderbot	Pre-K/K	At the most basic level, you can code Kinderbot to move using the directional arrows on the robot's head. But there are three different modes kids can explore: freely coding with the arrows, taking on challenges spoken to the kids by Kinderbot, or coding Kinderbot to do fun things using a secret codebook.
KIBO	Pre-K–5th Grade	KIBO engages children with both building with robotic parts (KIBO's hardware) and programming the robot to move with tangible programming blocks (KIBO's software). The kit contains easy-to-connect construction materials including wheels, motors, a light bulb, a variety of sensors, a wooden art platform, and more.

Figure 13.2. Young child holding a constructed KIBO robot with his code for the robot (created with tangible programming blocks) in front of him.

(a lab now based out of Boston College) and made commercially available through funding from the National Science Foundation (NSF) and a successful Kickstarter campaign. KIBO is unique compared to its counterparts on the commercial market because it engages children in both building with robotic parts (KIBO's hardware) and programming the robot to move with tangible programming blocks (KIBO's software). KIBO is designed based on years of child development research led by our mentor, Professor Marina Umaschi Bers, and is intended explicitly to meet the developmental needs of young children. The kit contains easy-to-connect construction materials including wheels, motors, a light bulb, a variety of sensors, a wooden art platform, and more (see Figure 13.2).

KIBO is programmed to move using a tangible programming language that consists of interlocking wooden programming blocks (see Figures 13.3 and 13.4). Using this block language, children are able to master increasingly complex programming concepts such as repeat loops, conditional

Figure 13.3. Some of the wooden programming blocks and parameters available for the KIBO robot.

Figure 13.4. A child holds up his block-based code for the KIBO robot. This code tells his robot to begin, turn on a red light, turn on a blue light, turn on a white light, play a recorded sound, shake, play another recorded sound, and then end.

if/else statements, and nested loops (e.g., a repeat inside of another repeat). These wooden blocks resemble familiar early childhood manipulatives such as alphabet blocks and contain no embedded electronics or digital components. Instead, KIBO's main body has an embedded scanner that scans the barcodes on the programming blocks in order to "read" the program the child has created. Once the program has been scanned, it is saved on the robot instantly. No interaction with a computer, tablet, or phone is required!

Along with these robotic and programming components, the KIBO kit also contains art platforms that can be used for children to personalize their projects with crafts materials and foster STEAM integration (see Figures 13.5, 13.6, and 13.7). Unlike KIBO, many robots for young children come out of the box already decorated to look like a toy or creature. For example, the Bee-Bot is designed to look like a bumblebee. Some of the other robots listed in Table 13.2 look like a caterpillar or a mouse. KIBO, on the other hand, does not look like much of anything until the child places their imagination on it. It does not have a face and is constructed of neutral colors and wooden materials. Like an unsculpted wad of Play-Doh, KIBO looks and feels different each time a child uses it. In this way, it is the ideal robotics kit to foster open-ended play and artistic exploration.

KIBO, and all of the other screen-free robots listed in Table 13.2, can be integrated into your curriculum in many different ways across a variety of interdisciplinary subjects—not just as part of a STEAM or technology unit. We will return to examples of this in the following chapter, which explores coding in the classroom and the idea of not just learning to code but coding to learn.

COMPUTER SCIENCE PICTURE BOOKS

From the most high-tech tool you might envision in an early childhood setting (robots), we move to perhaps the most foundational resource found in any early learning setting, both formal and informal: books. Books are a wonderful, low-cost, accessible way to begin talking about coding and building young children's interests in computer science. There are a growing number of fiction and nonfiction books that introduce computer science concepts in colorful, fun, and engaging ways (we provide a list of suggested STEAM books, including computer science themed books, in Appendix E). For example, *How to Code a Sandcastle* by Josh Funk follows the whimsical story of Pearl and her robot friend Pascal as they use fundamental computer coding concepts like sequences and loops to break down their sandcastle problem into small, manageable steps. Even younger learners can get introduced to how coding impacts our everyday lives in simple board books like *Baby Loves Coding* by Ruth Spiro.

Figures 13.5, 13.6, and 13.7. Different creations built with the KIBO robotics kit.

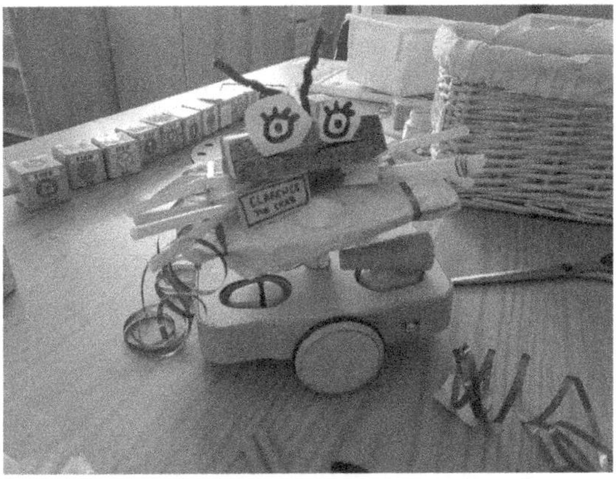

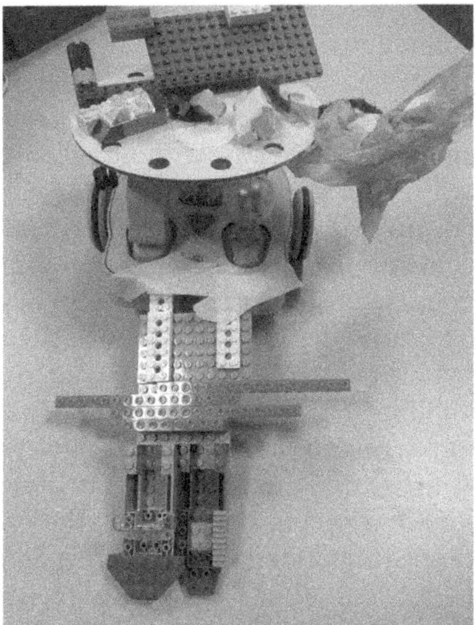

Books, what we might think of as the original "unplugged" method to learn through, have the power to build young children's curiosities, imagination, and even counter stereotypes about what fields like computer science or engineering are like. They can be offered during free-play periods, read aloud during full group gatherings, and suggested to parents and caregivers to continue exploring coding with their young children at home, without having to worry about learning a new app, technology, or device. Perhaps most exciting for educators, books can be used to spark longer-term explorations of STEAM topics and projects, including using storybook characters as "clients" in a problem-solving investigation (such as how to build an even sturdier home for the three little pigs).

CLOSING THOUGHTS

Today, "unplugged" computer science can mean a lot of different things to a lot of different people. We have explored the original movement along with the variations of tools, technologies, books, and games that allow young children to gain computer science skills without relying on tablets, computers, or other screens.

We also explored, and will continue to explore, screen-free robotics kits in early education contexts. We describe these kits to paint the full picture of what playful, screen-free STEAM can look like in early childhood settings and to shift educators' mindsets about what technology looks like. However, it is important to note that many of the robotics kits we have explored are cost-prohibitive for schools and individuals, even with grants, fundraising, and cheaper options continually being developed.

At its heart, CS Unplugged is an equalizer that allows *anyone, anywhere* to learn computer science concepts, regardless of their access to technology. We firmly believe this is important to broadening interest and participation in computer science and all STEAM fields. Technologies—screen free or otherwise—are just one way to explore STEAM in the early years. From books to paper crafts to in-person games, there are a wealth of resources to begin teaching these concepts to young children, even with nothing but your bodies and your imaginations!

CHAPTER 14

Coding in the Classroom

Coding supports playful learning in the early years by providing a creative outlet where children can design, think imaginatively, and utilize their problem-solving skills in order to complete projects that are personally meaningful to them and make them proud. When introduced in playful and open-ended ways, coding allows children to design their own games, stories, and interactive projects all while fostering creativity and self-expression. While many educators will gravitate toward "drill and skill" coding apps and screen-based programs, using the Playful STEAM Learning Framework can support educators with introducing coding in their classrooms in screen-free, playful, and developmentally appropriate ways.

Learning to code as an educational movement emerged into the national spotlight during the first Computer Science Education Week held in 2009, which later became Hour of Code in 2013 (see https://csedweek.org/about). That turned out to be a big year for computer science, as this same year New York City mayor Bill de Blasio launched the Tech Talent Pipeline, aiming to give hundreds of after-school programs access to free computer science learning materials from Google. Coding education gained even greater visibility at the national level in 2014, when then President Barack Obama very publicly wrote his first line of JavaScript and became one of over 100 million people worldwide to have participated in Code.org's Hour of Code event. Out of this publicity and funding came policies and frameworks related to computer science.

Today, that initiative has spurred education stakeholders and policymakers to launch computer science initiatives in schools all around the world. For example, New York City's Department of Education launched the Computer Science for All (CS4All) initiative to provide all students with access to computer science education by 2025 (NYC Department of Education, 2020). Finland, Japan, and the United Kingdom are part of a growing list of countries that now require coding as part of the national curriculum for students as young as 5 years old (Aalto University, 2015; BBC News, 2014; ST Office Tokyo, 2019). As a result, coding is no longer seen as a specialized skill for professional computer scientists but as a fundamental to 21st-century literacy, driving equity initiatives and innovation in education (Code.org, 2020).

One of the benefits of this international attention on computer science education is the availability of rigorous and evidence-based frameworks for coding and computation. The K–12 Computer Science Framework was one of the initial attempts to establish core concepts and practices for K–12 students (K–12 Computer Science Framework, 2016; CSTA, 2020). Developed through collaboration by organizations like Code.org, the Computer Science Teachers Association (CSTA), and the Association for Computing Machinery (ACM), the K–12 CS Framework emphasizes technological skills like programming and data analysis, as well as critical thinking skills such as computational reasoning and considering technology's impact on society.

Another popular resource is the Next Generation Science Standards (NGSS Lead States, 2013). While NGSS focuses on science education, its three-dimensional framework of science learning incorporates crosscutting and disciplinary content from computer science, as well as engineering and design practices. These standards encourage computational thinking and systems modeling as part of scientific inquiry and problem-solving processes.

Finally, the CSforALL Movement (not to be confused with NYC's CS4All initiative) is a grassroots national initiative with leaders from the Association of Computing Machinery (ACM), the College Board, the Computer Science Teachers Association (CSTA), and the National Center for Women & Information Technology (NCWIT), among other organizations (see www.csforall.org/about/). CSforALL aims to support the broad adoption of computer science in formal education by providing resources for schools and districts to implement equitable CS programs, prioritize teacher professional development, and form partnerships with community organizations.

SCREEN-FREE HOUR OF CODE RESOURCES

The Hour of Code is a 1-hour introduction to computer science, using fun tutorials to show that anybody can learn the basics. Whether you or your students are experienced coders or you all are setting out to explore coding and computer science for the very first time, Hour of Code has a wealth of resources to offer. People around the world often join the Hour of Code celebration during Computer Science Education Week (usually held in December), but you can do an Hour of Code any day of the year.

When most educators think of Hour of Code resources, they think of the digital activities and tutorials on the website (www.hourofcode.com). But it actually offers screen-free activities and resources as well. These offline activities help students develop computational thinking and problem-solving skills without the need for digital devices, making them ideal for classrooms with limited technology or for promoting balanced tech use. Examples of screen-free activities include paper-based coding challenges, unplugged lessons where students simulate coding with physical actions, and storytelling exercises that teach algorithmic thinking. These activities maintain the spirit of Hour of Code by ensuring that learners of all ages can access core computer science concepts, with or without digital tools. Screen-free activities (and all Hour of Code activities) can be found year-round on the Hour of Code website.

CONTEXTS FOR INTEGRATING CODING IN SCHOOL SETTINGS

Vignette: Coding a Robot with Videk and Mallory (Kindergarten)

"Argh, it's still not working!" Videk shouts at his partner. He is so frustrated he stomps away from the robot they are working on together and throws himself onto the beanbag chair in his classroom's Calming Corner. Videk's kindergarten teacher, Mr. Price, notices his frustration from across the room and walks over to Videk's partner, Mallory, who also looks a little sad. "I noticed your partner looks frustrated. Can you tell me what's going on?" Mallory shows Mr. Price the KIBO robot and the coding blocks they've been building. "Mr. Price, I know we're supposed to make this robot go forward on this line, but I think this one is broken. It keeps moving the wrong way." She shows Mr. Price their code, which reads: [Begin, Backward, Backward, Backward]. Mr. Price raises an eyebrow and taps his chin. "Hmm, that is tough. What have you already done to try and fix the problem?" Mallory explains that they checked the motors on the robot and made sure the path (a line of masking tape on the floor) was smooth with no obstacles in the way. Videk has been listening and now calls out, "You forgot that we also put on new wheels! This robot definitely needs new batteries!" Mr. Price nods and then says, "it sounds like you've done a good check on the hardware. Checking the batteries is a good solution, but first let's make sure to also check your software. Can you tell me about your code?"

Videk walks over as Mallory explains that they chose coding blocks with straight arrows to move the robot in a straight line. When Mr. Price asks which way the arrows are pointing, Videk says, "We know they aren't pointing the right way, but when we scanned the robot we spun the blocks upside down so it would work." Mr. Price pauses for a moment and says, "That is a really clever way to explain to a human friend how to move straight, but I think you're right that this robot doesn't understand things as well as you do. We need to be very specific. Maybe we can find another block that has the arrow pointing in the right direction, so you don't have to spin the program upside down? You can share blocks with other kids in the room if you can't find the one you're looking for." Mallory and Videk get to work looking for a [Forward] block while Mr. Price moves to another group to check on their progress.

Coding in the classroom is a delicate balance. You need to allow students the time and space to work through the hard fun that naturally comes with programming tasks while also juggling the demands of students' frustration tolerance, collaboration skills, and instructional needs, among all the other curriculum requirements and time constraints that come with a school setting. This section describes three of the most common ways that we've seen students successfully exposed to coding and computer science in school settings. All of these contexts allow for screen-free, computation-rich learning but require different kinds of planning and consideration on the part of the educator. Table 14.1 summarizes some common strategies used in these contexts. (These are examples, not hard-and-fast rules.)

Classroom Context: In this setting, educators can integrate coding into the daily curriculum, enhancing students' understanding of core concepts through interactive activities. The challenge of this environment is meeting the students' need for flexible and open-ended exploration of the tool or task while staying on pace to progress through the curricular unit. Research shows that coding tasks can support learning in other domains such as math, literacy, and science (Bers, 2021; Clements & Sarama, 2018; Kazakoff & Bers, 2012; Somuncu & Aslan, 2022). To improve your students' success, aim to select tasks that are closely aligned with overall learning goals.

Consider the general socio-emotional and executive functioning skills of your student group and design your task to allow as much creativity as possible while providing enough structure that *most of the group* can succeed. Coding tasks can be frustrating for first-time learners, so prepare them for the hard fun by praising effort and by modeling how to handle frustration. It can help to demonstrate any parts of the lesson that might be the same for everyone and to share examples for parts that invite creativity (Hattie, 2009). Many resources already exist for integrating coding into the early childhood curriculum, such as the *Coding as Another Language Curriculum*, developed by the DevTech Research Group, and *Coding, Robotics, and Engineering for Young Students*, originally developed by Northwestern University's Center for Talent Development (Bers et al., 2022; Gadzikowski, 2021).

Pairing students with partners can help them persevere when one or the other partner gets stuck, but even independent workers can benefit from structured times for teamwork and collaboration (e.g., share-out circle) to plan and iterate on their ideas. While it may not be necessary to evaluate your students, it can be helpful to have a clear and simple evaluation rubric to clarify the aspects of students' final projects that are most important to you, so that you can guide them back to a focus point if they are overwhelmed by the options or lost in details. Remember that anything you value can go onto a rubric, including collaboration, problem-solving, creative thinking, editing your work, and helping peers through the coding challenge (Bers, 2022). Finally, budget class time to share finished projects

Table 14.1. School-Based Contexts and Considerations for Screen-Free Coding

<table>
<tr><th>Contexts</th><th>Screen-Free Tools and Activities</th><th>Pedagogy</th><th>Instructional Strategies</th><th>Evaluation</th></tr>
<tr><td>Classroom</td><td rowspan="2">Screen-free tech kits (e.g., KIBO robot)
Collaborative board games
Open-ended group tasks (e.g., algorithmic thinking challenge)
Individual coding logic puzzles</td><td>Curriculum-aligned tasks (selected by teacher to build knowledge of a core concept)</td><td>Expert demonstration
Scaffolded exploration (e.g., worksheet-based)</td><td>Presentation or project deliverable
Rubric to guide student work</td></tr>
<tr><td>Club</td><td>Interest-aligned tasks (selected by teacher selected to build skill proficiency)</td><td>Scaffolded exploration
Semi-structured project prompt</td><td>Ongoing project and documentation
Informal student engagement and self-reflection</td></tr>
<tr><td>Computer Lab (or other “open studio”)</td><td>Screen-free tech kits (assumes prior exposure or clear instructions for independent work)
Individual coding logic puzzles</td><td>Open exploration
Sample finished or in-progress artifacts (selected by space facilitator to inspire curiosity)</td><td>Tutorials or project prompts provided at accessible level for student audience</td><td>No formal evaluation
Evidence of student ownership over coding process</td></tr>
</table>

in an enjoyable way, such as a low-stakes group presentation or a scheduled “play day” when everyone gets to try out each other’s projects. This is important for helping students stay on-task and work toward a meaningful and exciting end product.

Club Context: Coding clubs provide a more relaxed environment where interest-driven learning can drive activities and learning opportunities. Educators can select tasks that align with students’ interests and skill levels, encouraging self-directed exploration. A great way to start this conversation is to reserve time on the first day of the club to invite students to share ideas of what they want to do during club time or something they really hope to

Table 14.2. Curriculum-Aligned Examples of Screen-Free Coding Activities

Curriculum Topic	Screen-Free Coding Activity	Coding and Computational Thinking Content
Language Arts • Storytelling • Attending to details in stories and illustrations	*Story Sequencing*: Use picture cards to represent the sequence of a story. Students arrange the cards in the correct order, mimicking algorithmic thinking.	• Sequencing and order
Mathematics • Geometry • Spatial reasoning	*Program a Shape*: Students program a classmate, or a screen-free robot, holding a marker to move around butcher paper using directional commands (e.g., "move forward three steps, turn right, move forward two steps"). Challenge students to draw shapes with their coding instructions. For younger students, use making tape to make large shapes on the floor, and invite them to code their friend or their robot to "walk the shape," using very specific instructions.	• Logic and algorithmic thinking • Problem-solving
Art • Patterns and sequences • Properties of geometric shapes	*Make My Pattern*: Using pattern blocks, students create patterns and then describe the algorithm (instructions) to replicate the pattern to a friend. Extend to a creative arts activity of creating an image or mandala instead of a series (straight line) pattern of blocks, and giving coding-style instructions to a friend to recreate the artwork.	• Looping/repeating functions • Pattern logic • Attending to precision and following instructions
Physical Education • Dance and body coordination • Cultural dance and music	*Code a Dance*: Students create a "dance code" by writing down a sequence of movements (e.g., jump, spin, clap) and then performing them in order, or coding a screen-free robot to perform the dance moves. Have students invent their own dances or learn famous dances from cultures around the world.	• Sequencing • Algorithmic logic

(*continued*)

Table 14.2. *(continued)*

Curriculum Topic	Screen-Free Coding Activity	Coding and Computational Thinking Content
Social Studies • Maps and features of maps • Orienteering and navigation • Observation skills	*Nature Treasure Maps*: In an outdoor setting, students create or annotate a map of their environment, adding directions and movements to guide the reader. Have them add a legend with simple symbols for different actions (e.g., jump over a log, crawl under a branch). Students can try to follow each other's maps to find secret locations or treasures	• Symbol recognition (critical for learning coding languages) • Spatial and algorithmic thinking
Science / Engineering • Sturdy building • Science documentation	*Building Structures*: Using building blocks or LEGO, students design one or more structures based on specific criteria (e.g., height, stability) and explain the "code" behind their building choices to always make structures that meet the criteria.	• Problem-solving • Critical thinking • Design iteration

make or learn by the time the club cycle is over. In addition to flexibility in activity planning, clubs also provide opportunities to offer open-ended play prompts that allow for more creative direction and interpretation than a classroom project might. As long as they are roughly exploring the goals of coding logic, problem-solving, sequencing, or algorithmic thinking, there is probably no need to keep students focused on tasks or topics that don't interest them. You might find that they quickly develop their own playful and personally meaningful project ideas.

Evaluation in this context is likely to be informal and mainly for planning follow-up activities or sharing updates with families. For example, a club facilitator might notice that after playing a coding board game, many students are curious about the idea of looping patterns in codes. The following class might begin with a simple puzzle about loops to help the adult formatively assess children's prior knowledge and decide on the best ways to keep exploring repeat loops through games and activities. Since clubs also provide lots of free time and a community of peers with similar interests, clubs can emphasize student engagement and reflection on their process, fostering a sense of ownership and community among participants.

Computer Lab or Open Studio: This context promotes independent exploration of coding concepts through self-led activities, for example, playing with screen-free technology kits and working on logic puzzles. This is one of the more challenging spaces to support new learners, since materials and activity prompts have to be provided in a way that offers easy entry points for anyone who wants to play but might not have the benefit of ongoing community support, as with a classroom or club. Providing tasks with "low floors, wide walls, and high ceilings" is the best strategy to engage the widest population of learners without requiring deep background knowledge to play (Resnick & Silverman, 2005).

Facilitators can inspire curiosity by showcasing artifacts and providing accessible tutorials (Hennessey & Amabile, 2010). For example, a museum-style exhibit of a coding project started in a classroom, with pictures, student work, and a short video or poster that describes that coding challenge students worked on might inspire a different child to work independently on their own version of the same task. You could also design playful Reggio Emilia–inspired coding "provocations," such as a prompt on the wall that asks: "Can you close your eyes and walk across the room without hitting any furniture? Write down all the steps you think in your head as you go! Post your instructions on the bulletin board next to the other solutions."

In this context, evaluation focuses less on learning and more on student ownership and engagement in coding tasks. Encourage students to document their progress by celebrating finished and in-progress student-made projects visibly around the room. This builds an asynchronous community feeling and also lessens the pressure of sharing "perfect" work.

CONCLUDING THOUGHTS

Any school context offers unique opportunities to foster coding in different ways, but all are impactful ways to introduce coding in creative, exploratory, and self-directed ways for all students. Whether through structured classroom lessons, informal coding clubs, or independent exploration in a computer lab, coding provides students with essential problem-solving and computational thinking skills. By incorporating coding into everyday learning, educators can make abstract concepts tangible, encourage collaboration, build a foundation for future STEAM learning, and help empower students to be creators and not just consumers of their technology experiences.

Conclusion

Beyond Screen-Free STEAM

Play is at the heart of how young children grow, learn, socialize, and develop. Children's need for play is so powerful that it emerges even when there are no toys, limited resources, and in situations where adults do not actively encourage it (White, 2012). Children are naturally driven to play, and we hope through reading this book you have seen how play can be a core element of your educational practice, especially when it comes to STEAM. Each of STEAM's five subject domains (science, technology, engineering, arts, and mathematics) focuses on exploring curiosities, asking questions, creating new things, and solving problems. STEAM involves a process of inquiry, discovery, and creation that mirrors what happens in the play young children engage in every day.

Throughout this book, we discussed the Playful STEAM Learning Framework, which encourages a variety of different kinds of child-led and adult-scaffolded play experiences. The framework identifies three overarching play approaches, specific strategies educators can implement, as well as evaluation approaches that can be implemented in both formal and informal learning settings. When you are putting everything you have read into practice and are planning STEAM activities and curricula to implement, consider mindfully planning to foster the three types of play described in the Playful STEAM Learning Framework:

1. **Curiosity-Based Play** supports children's questions and helps develop their intellectual curiosity through play. Fostering curiosity-based play experiences in the context of the Playful STEAM Learning Framework can be accomplished by staying in tune to children's questions and ideas and offering materials and opportunities for children to explore them through different kinds of play and experimentation. Educators can celebrate their questions, for example, with an ongoing "Question Wall" to display questions that come up throughout the day. A major piece of supporting curiosity-based play is fostering a "curiosity cycle" where one discovery leads to new child-led questions to explore. Educators can remember to ask children things like "what does this

make you curious about exploring next?" when they complete a project or experiment.
2. **Child-Led Play** lets children take the lead in their playful learning experiences. As educators, you will still be supporting and scaffolding their learning experience. But child-led play in the context of the Playful STEAM Learning Framework means adults intervening less. It often means assuming the role of a co-learner or facilitator rather than an "instructor." In practice, this can mean asking guided questions, sharing your thoughts and observations, and making suggestions for students to deepen their learning by adding detail or complexity to their exploration. When it comes to planning your lessons and activities, it may mean building in opportunities for children to learn by doing on their own rather than learning by following step-by-step instructions or watching demonstrations.
3. **Authentic Play** supports children engaging in learning that is personally and culturally meaningful to them. Facilitating authentic play in the context of the Playful STEAM Learning Framework means encouraging youth voice and choice by offering different ways for children to guide their own playful learning experiences. From what to explore, to what materials to use, to how students would like to showcase or share their knowledge, there are many ways that educators can give young children an active voice in their learning process. Part of authentic playful learning is offering meaningful opportunities for them to make connections with what they are learning to their family, interests, and lives outside of school. It also means giving children authentic opportunities to share their learning and to give and receive recognition from peers and other adults—all key elements of fostering a positive STEAM identity.

The threeplay approaches summarized above, which can be relevant to both STEAM and non-STEAM domains, are vehicles to support the four pillars of the Playful STEAM Learning Framework: (1) **P**ersevering through hard fun, (2) **L**istening to children's ideas, (3) **A**ctively supporting inclusion, and (4) Saying **Y**es to open-ended sensory play. Recall that we use the acronym "**PLAY**" to remember these four pillars. Moreover, we use this acronym as an active reminder that play is a crucial piece of learning and development. Play, joy, laughter, and discovery are at the heart of all of the most powerful early learning experiences.

Throughout this book, we have also seen many different examples of types of STEAM play. This has included board games, open-ended experimentation, sensory play, messy play, dramatic play, and more. There is no one "right" or "wrong" way to encourage STEAM play. We hope you have seen that there are many different ways to approach STEAM play, ranging in levels of structure, adult involvement, preparation, and resources needed. There is a type of STEAM play that can fit any kind of curricular goal and in any early childhood learning setting, both formal and informal.

THE POWER OF STEAM

While the framework we present could be applied to support many different types of playful learning, we focus on STEAM because of the importance of exposing children to positive STEAM experiences from an early age. Young children are naturally curious about the world around them, and hands-on, playful STEAM learning can build on this curiosity and allow for amazing discoveries to take place. We also know that early childhood is a critical time to begin reaching all young children, particularly girls and other groups historically excluded from the sciences, with positive STEAM experiences to counter stereotypes, pique their interests, and build confidence to support their STEAM learning for years to come (Sullivan, 2019).

We also focus on STEAM due to the rising nature of screen-based interventions for STEAM learning, particularly with the increased international focus on computer science education. We take a screen-free approach with our examples of the Playful STEAM Learning Framework to combat the popular fallacy that you cannot teach core technology, coding, and engineering concepts and practices without using screens.

While the framework could also be applied to screen-based play, we have focused on screen-free play and learning in this book. As more and more screen-based tools are being used in schools for assessment, skills practice, and remediation in all domains, including math and literacy, the urgency is heightened for tools like the Playful STEAM Learning Framework, to support practical and evidence-based uses of unplugged play as an intentional approach to children's education.

TRANSITIONING FROM SCREEN-FREE TO SCREEN-BASED STEAM

Although we have focused on screen-free STEAM, we know that there are many benefits to quality screen-based STEAM learning programs. This is especially true when children are ready to explore more advanced coding, animation, and digital design projects. After mastering the unplugged coding concepts and tools introduced in this book, for example, children in early and late elementary school may wish to move on to block-based programming languages on a computer or tablet.

Block-based programming is coding within a programming language where instructions are mainly represented as blocks (in contrast to text-based programming that adults or older youth might use, which is oriented around text commands). Block-based languages simplify the syntax of a programming language by removing (or limiting) text and focusing on making programming visual and approachable for young users—as well as novices of any age—to explore coding. These languages allow users to write code in a similar fashion to connecting puzzle pieces: Only pieces that are meant to work together will fit together, eliminating potential syntax errors and freeing up cognitive space for children to explore creative expression, storytelling, design, and more.

There are many examples of block-based programming languages including Blockly (for ages 6+) and Scratch (for ages 8+). The Scratch programming language, developed by the MIT LifeLong Kindergarten Group for youth around ages 8–16, is one of the most widely used educational programming languages for children. In order to bring the benefits of Scratch to younger children, the DevTech Research Group, the MIT Lifelong Kindergarten Group, and the Playful Invention Company collaborated to develop ScratchJr with funding from the National Science Foundation.

ScratchJr is an introductory programming tool for children ages 5–7 that allows young children to explore introductory coding concepts such as algorithms, debugging, and the design process in a fun and playful way (Bers, 2017). As a classic example of block-based programming, ScratchJr allows children to drag and drop blocks to create a program for each character they select. Children snap together motion, sound, looks, and communication blocks to program their own stories and games. The application supports English literacy skills (and other left-to-right written languages) by creating scripts in a horizontal manner instead of the top-to-bottom approach used in Scratch. Furthermore, children can code their stories with up to four "pages" in each project, allowing them to script a beginning, middle, and end. The ScratchJr blocks were created to look like puzzle pieces with specific syntactic goals. Blocks to end a program (e.g., "End" and "Repeat Forever") have a rounded edge on the right side, while blocks that start a script (e.g., "Start on Green Flag") have a rounded edge on the left side. The blocks for middle scripts are cut in a way that they can be snapped together to form a complete and syntactically correct programming script.

Most importantly, unlike many other "drill and skill" style apps, ScratchJr can be described as a technological "playground" for young children (Bers, 2012). Like a playground, the environment is open-ended and allows for child-directed exploration, play, and learning. ScratchJr users are encouraged to learn by experimenting, to try out new programming blocks, to express themselves creatively and artistically, to tell stories, and to collaborate with peers while having fun. ScratchJr does not teach concepts through "challenge levels" or gaining points. Instead, it is an open-ended interface that promotes creativity, curiosity, and child-led playful learning.

When educators are choosing digital programs to supplement the screen-free STEAM activities and approaches described in this book, we encourage them to seek out open-ended and playful interfaces whenever possible. This means looking beyond highly popular but often very structured learning apps, to offer digital tools that will build on the concepts and skills learned in unplugged settings by engaging children as *creators* of their digital experience, not just *consumers* of it. These may include open-ended programming languages, movie-editing software, photo-editing software, stop-motion animation apps, and more.

WHAT COMES AFTER EARLY CHILDHOOD STEAM?

We align with researchers, educators, and advocates who encourage more opportunities for open-ended, unstructured play in learning settings for children. We strongly believe this is important at the toddler and preschool level, where we are delighted to see that many play-based programs are still standing strong. We also urgently call for more opportunities for play in formal elementary (and beyond) school settings, where play is progressively phased out in favor of rigorous, structured, achievement-oriented academic programs.

As our society becomes increasingly digital, we know it is important for our youngest learners to explore and understand the technological world they are growing up in. Understanding coding, building computational thinking skills, and exploring foundational engineering concepts are critical for young children to gain the competence and confidence they need to meaningfully engage with these fields in later years. However, gaining these skills and competencies *does not* have to happen exclusively through digital, screen-based, technological tools. At the early childhood and early elementary school level, children *can* gain a foundational understanding of these fields through books, hands-on experimentation, craft-based projects, projects that integrate the arts, and most importantly, through play.

As children grow and continue to pursue interests in STEAM, they may "graduate" to digital interfaces. Or educators may choose to intersperse the use of digital and non-digital tools in their teaching practice. However you choose to approach STEAM education, do not forget the value of play. We hope after reading this book you will not be fooled by the term "playful" STEAM, and you will know that through playfully engaging in "hard fun," children's brains are engaged in hard work. Through this type of play, children are not learning to get the right answers but to ask the right questions. They are learning to explore, experiment, and question the world around them rather than accepting the status quo. And they are gaining the foundational STEAM skills they need to be active and engaged members of 21st-century society.

References

Aalto University. (2015, December 14). Finland is a pioneer in teaching coding at schools in Europe. https://www.aalto.fi/en/news/finland-is-a-pioneer-in-teaching-coding-at-schools-in-europe

Ackermann, E. (2001). Piaget's constructivism, Papert's constructionism: What's the difference? *Future of Learning Group Publication*, *5*(3), 438.

Alexandre, S., Xu, Y., Washington-Nortey, M., & Chen, C. (2022). Informal STEM learning for young children: A systematic literature review. *International Journal of Environmental Research and Public Health*, *19*(14), 8299.

Allen, P. J., Noam, G., Little, T. D., Fukuda, E., Chang, R., Gorrall, B., & Waggenspack, L. (2016). *Afterschool & STEM system building evaluation 2016*. PEAR Institute & Institute for Measurement, Methodology, Analysis, and Policy. https://www.thepearinstitute.org/afterschool-stem-evaluation-2016

Allen-Handy, A., Ifill, V., Schaar, R. Y., Rogers, M., & Woodard, M. (2020). Black girls STEAMing through dance: Inspiring STEAM literacies, STEAM identities, and positive self-concept. In K. Thomas & D. Huffman (Eds.), *Challenges and opportunities for transforming from STEM to STEAM education* (pp. 198–219). IGI Global.

Allina, B. (2018). The development of STEAM educational policy to promote student creativity and social empowerment. *Arts Education Policy Review, 119*(2), 77–87.

American Montessori Society. (2013). *What is Montessori education?* https://amshq.org/About-Montessori/What-Is-Montessori

Archer, L., Moote, J., Francis, B., DeWitt, J., & Yeomans, L. (2017). The "exceptional" physics girl: A sociological analysis of multimethod data from young women aged 10–16 to explore gendered patterns of post-16 participation. *American Educational Research Journal, 54*(1), 88–126. https://doi.org/10.3102/0002831216678379

Artiles, A. (2011). Toward an interdisciplinary understanding of educational equity and difference. *Educational Researcher*, *40*(9), 431–445. https://doi.org/10.3102/0013189X11429391

BBC. (2024). *Computer science*. BBC Bitesize. https://www.bbc.co.uk/bitesize/subjects/zvc9q6f

BBC News. (2014, September 1). *Pupils begin "tough" new national curriculum.* https://www.bbc.com/news/education-28987787

Becker, C., Lauterbach, G., Spengler, S., Dettweiler, U., & Mess, F. (2017). Effects of regular classes in outdoor education settings: A systematic review on students' learning, social and health dimensions. *International Journal of Environmental Research and Public Health, 14*(5), 485.

Bell, P., Lewenstein, B., Shouse, A., & Feder, M. (2009). Learning science in informal environments: People, places, and pursuits. *Museums & Social Issues, 4*(1), 113–124.

Bell, T., Witten, I. H., & Fellows, M. (1999). *Computer science unplugged: Off-line activities and games for all ages.* CS Unplugged. https://classic.csunplugged.org/documents/books/english/unplugged-book-v1.pdf

Bequette, J. W., & Bequette, M. B. (2015). A place for art and design education in the STEM conversation. *Art Education, 65*(2), 40–47.

Berger, W. (2014). *A more beautiful question: The power of inquiry to spark breakthrough ideas.* Bloomsbury Publishing USA.

Bers, M. (Ed.). (2021). *Teaching computational thinking and coding to young children.* IGI Global. https://www.igi-global.com/book/teaching-computational-thinking-coding-young/262496

Bers, M., Ponte, I., Juelich, K., Viera, A., & Schenker, J. (2002). Teachers as designers: Integrating robotics in early childhood education. *Information Technology in Childhood Education, 2002*(1), 123–145.

Bers, M., Seddighin, S., & Sullivan, A. (2013). Ready for robotics: Bringing together the T and E of STEM in early childhood teacher education. *Journal of Technology and Teacher Education, 21*(3), 355–377.

Bers, M. U. (2008). *Blocks to robots: Learning with technology in the early childhood classroom.* Teachers College Press.

Bers, M. U. (2012). *Designing digital experiences for positive youth development: From playpen to playground.* Oxford University Press.

Bers, M. U. (2017). *Coding as a playground: Programming and computational thinking in the early childhood classroom* (1st ed.). Routledge.

Bers, M. U. (2018, September). Coding as a literacy for the 21st century. *Education Week.* https://www.edweek.org/education/opinion-coding-as-a-literacy-for-the-21st-century/2018/01

Bers, M. U. (2020). *Coding as a playground: Programming and computational thinking in the early childhood* (2nd ed.). Routledge.

Bers, M. U., Govind, M., & Relkin, E. (2022). Coding as another language: Computational thinking, robotics and literacy in first and second grade. In A. Yadav & U. Berthelsen (Eds.), *Computational thinking in preK-5: Empirical evidence for integration and future directions* (pp. 30–38). ACM, New York, NY, USA.

Boy, G. A. (2013, August). From STEM to STEAM: Toward a human-centred education, creativity & learning thinking. In *Proceedings of the 31st European conference on cognitive ergonomics* (pp. 1–7). https://dl.acm.org/doi/10.1145/2501907.2501934

Brackmann, C. P., Román-González, M., Robles, G., Moreno-León, J., Casali, A., & Barone, D. (2017, November). Development of computational thinking skills through unplugged activities in primary school. In *Proceedings of the 12th workshop on primary and secondary computing education* (pp. 65–72). https://dl.acm.org/doi/10.1145/3137065.3137069

Brannon, M., & Novak, E. (2019). Coding success through math intervention in an elementary school in rural Amish country. *Journal of Computer Science Integration*, 2(2), 1–10. https://doi.org/10.26716/jcsi.2019.02.2.1

Bresler, L. (Ed.). (2007). *International handbook of research in arts education* (Vol. 16). Springer Science & Business Media.

Bronson, P., & Merryman, A. (2010, July 10). The creativity crisis. *Newsweek.* https://www.newsweek.com/creativity-crisis-74665

Brosterman, N. (1997). *Inventing kindergarten.* Abrams.

Broughton, A., & McClary, M. B. (2020). Creating a culturally responsive STEAM curriculum. *Teaching Young Children, 13*(2), 8–12.

Brown, S. L., & Vaughan, C. (2009). *Play: How it shapes the brain, opens the imagination, and invigorates the soul.* Penguin.

Burghardt, G. M. (2011). Defining and recognizing play. In A. D. Pellegrini (Ed.), *The Oxford handbook of the development of play* (pp. 9–18). Oxford University Press.

Busteed, B., & Sorenson, S. (2015). Many students lack access to computer science learning. Gallup Blog. https://www.gallup.com/education/243416/students-lack-access-computer-science-learning.aspx

Caiman, C., & Lundegård, I. (2018). Young children's imagination in science education and education for sustainability. *Cultural Studies of Science Education, 13*(3), 687–705.

Caldera, Y. M., Culp, A. M., O'Brien, M., Truglio, R. T., Alvarez, M., & Huston, A. C. (1999). Children's play preferences, construction play with blocks, and visual-spatial skills: Are they related? *International Journal of Behavioral Development, 23*(4), 855–872.

Cardinot, A., & Fairfield, J. A. (2019). Game-based learning to engage students with physics and astronomy using a board game. *International Journal of Game-Based Learning, 9*(1), 42–57.

Cardinot, A., McCauley, V., & Fairfield, J. A. (2022). Designing physics board games: A practical guide for educators. *Physics Education, 57*(3), 035006.

Carlone, H. B., & Johnson, A. (2007). Understanding the science experiences of successful women of color: Science identity as an analytic lens. *Journal of Research in Science Teaching, 44*(8), 1187–1218. https://doi.org/10.1002/tea.20237

Carlone, H. B., Scott, C. M., & Lowder, C. (2014). Becoming (less) scientific: A longitudinal study of students' identity work from elementary to middle school science. *Journal of Research in Science Teaching, 51*(7), 836–869. https://doi.org/10.1002/tea.21150

Casey, T., Robertson, J., Abel, J., Cairns, M., Caldwell, L., & Campbell, K. (2016). Loose parts play. Inspiring Scotland. https://inspiringscotland.org.uk/wp-content/uploads/2017/03/Loose-Parts-Play-web.pdf

CDC. (2018). Act early milestone checklist. Centers for Disease Control and Prevention. https://www.cdc.gov/ncbddd/actearly/milestones/index.html

Cejka, E., Rogers, C., & Portsmore, M. (2006). Kindergarten robotics: Using robotics to motivate math, science, and engineering literacy in elementary school. *International Journal of Engineering Education, 22*(4), 711.

Charara, J., Miller, E. A., & Krajcik, J. (2021). Knowledge in use: Designing for play in kindergarten science contexts. *Journal of Leadership, Equity, and Research, 7*(1), n1.

Chaudron, S., Di Gioia, R., & Gemo, M. (2019). Safety issues in young children's digital literacy practices at home. In O. Erstad, R. Flewitt, B. Kümmerling-Meibauer, & Í. S. P. Pereira (Eds.), *The Routledge handbook of digital literacies in early childhood* (pp. 134–145). Routledge.

Chawla, L. (2009). Growing up green: Becoming an agent of care for the natural world. *Journal of Developmental Processes*, *4*(1), 6–23.

Chen, S. Y., Tsai, J. C., Liu, S. Y., & Chang, C. Y. (2021). The effect of a scientific board game on improving creative problem solving skills. *Thinking Skills and Creativity, 41*, Article 100921. https://www.sciencedirect.com/science/article/abs/pii/S187118712100136X?via%3Dihub

Clements, D. H. (1999). The future of educational computing research: The case of computer programming. *Information Technology in Childhood Education Annual, 1999*(1), 147–179.

Clements, D. H., & Sarama, J. (2018). *Learning and teaching early math: The learning trajectories approach*. Routledge.

Coalition for Science After School (March, 2007). *Blueprint for action*. https://archive.informalscience.org/science-after-school-blueprint-action-2007

Code.org. (2020). State of computer science education: Illuminating disparities. https://code.org/assets/advocacy/stateofcs/2020_state_of_cs.pdf

Code.org, CSTA, & ECEP Alliance. (2024). 2024 State of computer science education. https://advocacy.code.org/stateofcs

Computer Science Teachers Association (CSTA). (2020). Standards Alignment Review. https://www.csteachers.org/page/standards

Conel, J. L. (1967). *The postnatal development of the human cerebral cortex*. Harvard University Press. (Original work published 1939)

Cordes, C., & Miller, E. (Eds.). (2000). *Fool's gold: A critical look at computers in childhood*. Alliance for Childhood.

Correia, M., Ribeirinha, T., Beirante, D., Santos, R., Ramos, L., Dias, I. S., Luís, H., Catela, D., Galinha, S., Arrais, A., Portelada, A., Pinto, P., Simões, V., Ferreira, R., Franco, S., & Martins, M. C. (2024). Outdoor STEAM education: Opportunities and challenges. *Education Sciences*, *14*(7), 688. https://doi.org/10.3390/educsci14070688

Council on Communications and Media. (2016). Media and young minds. *Pediatrics, 138*(5), e20162591.

Deans, J., & Wright, S. (2021). STEAM through sensory-based action-reaction learning. In C. Cohrssen & S. Garvis (Eds.), *Embedding STEAM in early childhood education and care* (pp. 135–153). Palgrave Macmillan.

Denning, P. J., & Tedre, M. (2019a). *Computational thinking*. MIT Press.

Denning, P. J., & Tedre, M. (2019b). Thinking like a computer. *American Scientist, 107*(3), 187–189.

Dinamani, P., & Shibley, R. (2023, April 25). Why aren't smartphones designed for a woman's hand size? *Digital Trends*. https://www.digitaltrends.com/mobile/smartphone-size-design-for-woman-hand/

Dong, C., & Xu, Q. (2021). Pre-service early childhood teachers' attitudes and intentions: Young children's use of ICT. *Journal of Early Childhood Teacher Education*, *42*(3), 203–218.

Dougherty, D. (2013). The maker mindset. In M. Honey & D. E. Kanter (Eds.), *Design make play: Growing the next generation of STEM innovators* (pp. 7–11). Routledge.

Downey, S., Hayes, N., & O'Neill, B. (2007). *Play and technology for children aged 4–12. Centre for Social and Educational Research*. Dublin Institute of Technology, Office of the Minister for Children, Government of Ireland.

Duffy, B. (2007). *All about . . . messy play. The Early Years Foundation Stage Primary National Strategy*. Department of Education: London. https://www.littlestarnursery.co.uk/wp-content/uploads/2015/09/importance-of-messy-play.pdf

Edwards, C. (2011). *The hundred languages of children: The Reggio Emilia experience in transformation*. ABC-CLIO.

Eisner, E. W. (2002). *The arts and the creation of mind*. Yale University Press.

Engel, S. (2021, February 23). Many kids ask fewer questions when they start school. Here's how we can foster their curiosity. *Time*. https://time.com/5941608/schools-questions-fostering-curiousity/

Falk, J. H., & Dierking, L. D. (2010). School is not where most Americans learn most of their science. *American Scientist*, *98*(6), 486–493

Fancsali, C. (2022). CS4All: Examining equity in computer science access and participation in NYC schools. Research Alliance for New York City Schools.

Farrell, T. S. C. (2002). Lesson planning. In T. S. C. Farrell (Ed.), *Planning lessons and units* (pp. 1–22). University of Michigan Press.

Fermin, C., Perez, M., Obee, A. F., & Hart, K. C. (2024). Benefits of time spent outdoors in early childhood education: A systematic review. *FIU Undergraduate Research Journal*, *2*(1), 6.

Fessakis, G., Gouli, E., & Mavroudi, E. (2013). Problem solving by 5–6 years old kindergarten children in a computer programming environment: A case study. *Computers & Education*, *63*, 87–97.

Fisher, K., Hirsh-Pasek, K., Golinkoff, R. M., Singer, D. G., & Berk, L. (2011). Playing around in school: Implications for learning and educational policy. In A. D. Pellegrini (Ed.), *The Oxford handbook of the development of play* (pp. 341–360). Oxford University Press.

Fleer, M. (2009). Supporting scientific conceptual consciousness or learning in "a roundabout way" in play-based contexts. *International Journal of Science Education*, *31*(8), 1069–1089.

Fowler, B., & Vegas, E. (2021). *How England implemented its computer science education program*. Center for Universal Education at the Brookings Institution. https://www.brookings.edu/wp-content/uploads/2021/01/How-England-implemented-its-computer-science-education-program.pdf

Fung, C. K. H., & Cheng, D. P. W. (2012). Consensus or dissensus? Stakeholders' views on the role of play in learning. *Early Years*, *32*(1), 17–33.

Gadzikowski, A. (2021). *Coding robotics and [Engineering] for young students: A tech beginnings curriculum, Grades Pre-K-2*. Routledge.

Gandini, L. (Ed.). (2005). *In the spirit of the studio: Learning from the atelier of Reggio Emilia*. Teachers College Press.

Gay, G. (2000). *Culturally responsive teaching: Theory, research, and practice*. Teachers College Press.

Gerber, B. L., Cavallo, A. M., & Marek, E. A. (2001). Relationships among informal learning environments, teaching procedures and scientific reasoning ability. *International Journal of Science Education*, *23*(5), 535–549.

Gilreath, A. (2022). *In elementary classrooms, demand grows for play-based learning*. Hechinger Report. https://hechingerreport.org/in-elementary-classrooms-demand-grows-for-play-based-learning/

Ginsburg, K. R., Committee on Communications, & Committee on Psychosocial Aspects of Child and Family Health. (2007). The importance of play in promoting healthy child development and maintaining strong parent-child bonds. *Pediatrics, 119*(1), 182–191.

Girl Scout Research Institute. (2022). *The impact of Girl Scout STEM programming*. Girl Scouts of the United States. https://www.girlscouts.org/content/dam/gsusa/forms-and-documents/about/research/GSUSA_GSRI_2022_The-Impact-of-Girl-Scout-STEM-Programming-Full-Report.pdf

Glatthorn, A. A., Boschee, F., Whitehead, B. M., & Boschee, B. F. (2018). *Curriculum leadership: Strategies for development and implementation*. Sage.

Glenberg, A. M., Gutierrez, T., Levin, J. R., Japuntich, S., & Kaschak, M. P. (2004). Activity and imagined activity can enhance young children's reading comprehension. *Journal of Educational Psychology, 96*(3), 424–436.

Gooley, T. (2014). *How to connect with nature* (Vol. 2). Pan Macmillan.

Gooley, T. (2016). *How to read water: Clues and patterns from puddles to the sea*. The Experiment.

Gopnik, A., Meltzoff, A. N., & Kuhl, P. K. (1999). *The scientist in the crib: Minds, brains, and how children learn*. William Morrow.

Gray, P. (2013). *Free to learn: Why unleashing the instinct to play will make our children happier, more self-reliant, and better students for life*. Basic Books.

Griffin, J. (2009, March 10). Academics like to play with Barbies, too. *Pacific Standard*. https://psmag.com/social-justice/academics-like-to-play-with-barbies-too-3898/

Hachey, A. C. (2020). Success for all: Fostering early childhood STEM identity. *Journal of Research in Innovative Teaching & Learning*, 13(1), 135–139.

Hakkarainen, P. (2008). The challenges and possibilities of a narrative learning approach in the Finnish early childhood education system. *International Journal of Educational Research, 47*(5), 292–300.

Hartman, S. L., & Dani, D. (2020). Full STEAM ahead: Creating interdisciplinary informal learning opportunities for early childhood teacher candidates. *Journal of STEM Teacher Education, 54*(1), 3.

Hashim, N. H., Harun, N. O., Ariffin, N. A., & Abdullah, N. A. C. (2024). Gamification using board game approach in science education—A systematic review. *Journal of Advanced Research in Applied Sciences and Engineering Technology, 33*(3), 73–85. https://doi.org/10.37934/araset.33.3.7385

Hattie, J. (2009). *Visible learning: A synthesis of over 800 meta-analyses relating to achievement*. Routledge.

Hawkins, M. R. (2005). *Becoming a student: Identity work and academic literacies in early schooling. Tesol Quarterly*, *39*(1), 59–80.

Hebb, D. O. (1949–2005). *The organization of behavior: A neuropsychological theory*. Psychology Press.

Hennessey, B. A., & Amabile, T. M. (2010). Creativity. *Annual Review of Psychology, 61*, 569–598.

Hirsh-Pasek, K., Golinkoff, R. M., Berk, L. E., & Singer, D. (2009). *A mandate for playful learning in preschool: Applying the scientific evidence*. Oxford University Press.

Honey, M., & Kanter, D. E. (Eds.). (2013). *Design, make, play: Growing the next generation of science innovators*. Routledge.

Hooft Graafland, J. (2018). *New technologies and 21st century children: Recent trends and outcomes*. OECD Education Working Papers, No. 179, OECD Publishing, Paris. https://doi.org/10.1787/e071a505-en

Howard, K. E., & Havard, D. D. (2019). Advanced Placement (AP) computer science principles: Searching for equity in a two-tiered solution to underrepresentation. *Journal of Computer Science Integration*, *2*(1), 1–15. https://doi.org/10.26716/jcsi.2019.01.1.1

Howard, N. R., & Howard, K. E. (2020). *Coding+Math: Strengthen K-5 math skills with computer science*. International Society for Technology in Education.

Hsu, Y. C., Baldwin, S., & Ching, Y. H. (2017). Learning through making and maker education. *TechTrends, 61*(6), 589–594.

Huang, T. J. (2017). Imitating the brain with neurocomputer a "new" way towards artificial general intelligence. *International Journal of Automation and Computing, 14*(5), 520–531.

Hughes, F. P. (2021). *Children, play, and development*. Sage.

Hughes, R., & Schellinger, J., (2023). Gatekeepers to Science and Engineering: Informal Science and Engineering Educator's Role in Positioning and Recognizing Girls' Identity Performances. *International Journal of Informal Science and Environmental Education, 3(*1)

K–12 Computer Science Framework. (2016). http://www.k12cs.org.

Kitchen, J. A., Sonnert, G., & Sadler, P. M. (2018). The impact of college- and university-run high school summer programs on students' end of high school STEM career aspirations. *Science Education, 102*(3), 529–547. https://onlinelibrary.wiley.com/doi/10.1002/sce.21332

Kashdan, T. B., Sherman, R. A., Yarbro, J., & Funder, D. C. (2013). How are curious people viewed and how do they behave in social situations? From the perspectives of self, friends, parents, and unacquainted observers. *Journal of personality*, *81*(2), 142–154.

Kazakoff, E., Sullivan, A., & Bers, M. U. (2013). The effect of a classroom-based intensive robotics and programming workshop on sequencing ability in early childhood. *Early Childhood Education Journal, 41*(4), 245–255. https://doi.org/10.1007/s10643-012-0554-5

Kazakoff, E. R., & Bers, M. U. (2012). Programming in a robotics context in the kindergarten classroom: The impact on sequencing skills. *Journal of Educational Multimedia and Hypermedia, 21*(4), 371–391.

Kennedy, T. J., & Tunnicliffe, S. D. (Eds.). (2022). *Play and STEM education in the early years*. Springer.

Kim, A. Y., Sinatra, G. M., & Seyranian, V. (2018). Developing a STEM identity among young women: A social identity perspective. *Review of Educational Research*, *20*(10), 1–37.

Kornelaki, A. C., & Plakitsi, K. (2018). Thunderbolt hunt. Educational program for students from 5 to 9 years old in the Archaeological Museum of Ioannina. *World Journal of Education*, *8*(4), 87–101.

Krasnor, L. R., & Pepler, D. J. (1980). The study of children's play: Some suggested future directions. *New Directions for Child and Adolescent Development, 1980*(9), 85–95.

Küçükşen Öner, F., Cetin-Dindar, A., & Sarı, H. (2024). I arrived at the sun! Developing an educational board game with the collaboration of pre-service art and pre-service science teachers. *European Journal of Education, 59*(2), Article e12629. https://doi.org/10.1111/ejed.12629

Kuh, L. P. (Ed.). (2014). *Thinking critically about environments for young children: Bridging theory and practice*. Teachers College Press.

Kyriacou, C. (2007). *Essential teaching skills* (3rd ed.). Nelson Thornes.

Ladson-Billings, G. (1995). But that's just good teaching! The case for culturally relevant pedagogy. *Theory into Practice, 34*(3), 159–165. https://www.tandfonline.com/doi/abs/10.1080/00405849509543675

Ladson-Billings, G. (2012, April). Toward a theory of culturally relevant pedagogy. *American Educational Research Journal, 32*(3). https://doi.org/10.3102/00028312032003465

Larimore, R. A. (2020). *Establishing a nature-based preschool: Successful strategies for early childhood educators*. Gryphon House.

Lee, K., Sullivan, A., & Bers, M. U. (2013). Collaboration by design: Using robotics to foster social interaction in kindergarten. *Computers in the Schools, 30*(3), 271–281.

Lillard, A. (2010). Montessori and playful learning. *American Journal of Play, 2*(2), 157–186.

Lilley, I. M. (1967). *Friedrich Froebel: A selection from his writings*. Cambridge University Press.

Liu, C., Solis, S. L., Jensen, H., Hopkins, E. J., Neale, D., Zosh, J. M., Hirsh-Pasek, K., & Whitebread, D. (2017, November). *Neuroscience and learning through play: A review of the evidence* (research summary). The LEGO Foundation. https://akcesedukacja.pl/images/dokumenty-pdf/Insight_and_Research/LEGO-Foundation---Neuroscience-and-learning-through-play-2017.pdf

Lockhart, S. (2010). Play: An important tool for cognitive development. *Extensions Curriculum Newsletter from HighScope, 24*(3), 1–8.

Lodi, M., & Martini, S. (2021). Computational thinking, between Papert and Wing. *Science & Education, 30*(4), 883–908.

Louv, R. (2008). *Last child in the woods: Saving our children from nature-deficit disorder.* Algonquin Books.

Lynch, M. (2015). More play, please: The perspective of kindergarten teachers on play in the classroom. *American Journal of Play, 7*(3), 347–370.

Madill, H., Campbell, R. G., Cullen, D. M., Armour, M. A., Einsiedel, A. A., Ciccocioppo, A. L., Sherman, J., Stewin, L. L., Varnhagen, S., Montgomerie, T. C., Rothwell, C. J., & Coffin, W. L. (2007). Developing career commitment in STEM-related fields: Myth versus reality. In R. J. Burke & M. C. Mattis (Eds.), *Women and minorities in science, technology, engineering and mathematics: Upping the numbers* (pp. 210–244). Edward Elgar.

Madkins, T. C., Howard, N. R., & Freed, N. (2020). Engaging equity pedagogies in computer science learning environments. *Journal of Computer Science Integration, 3*(2), Article 2.

Madkins, T. C., Martin, A., Ryoo, J., Scott, K. A., Goode, J., Scott, A., & McAlear, F. (2019). Culturally relevant computer science pedagogy: From theory to practice. 2019 Research on Equity and Sustained Participation in Engineering, Computing, and Technology (RESPECT) Conference Proceedings, Minneapolis, MN (pp. 1–4). https://doi.org/10.1109/respect46404.2019.8985773

Maguth, B. M. (2012). In defense of the social studies: Social studies programs in STEM education. *Social Studies Research and Practice*, 7(2), 65–90.

Margolis, J., & Goode, J. (2016). Ten lessons for CS for All. *ACM Inroads*, *7*(4), 52–56. https://doi.org/10.1145/2988236

Markert, L. R. (1996). Gender related to success in science and technology. *Journal of Technology Studies, 22*(2), 21–29.

Martin, L. M. (2004). An emerging research framework for studying informal learning and schools. *Science Education*, *88*(S1), S71–S82.

Mascolo, M. F., & Fischer, K. W. (2005). Constructivist theories. In M. H. Bornstein, L. Davidson, C. L. M. Keyes, & K. A. Moore (Eds.), *Cambridge Encyclopedia of Child Development* (pp. 49–63). Cambridge University Press.

Masoumi, D. (2020). Situating ICT in early childhood teacher education. *Education and Information Technologies, 26*(3), 1–18.

Master, A., Cheryan, S., Moscatelli, A., & Meltzoff, A. N. (2017). Programming experience promotes higher STEM motivation among first-grade girls. *Journal of Experimental Child Psychology*, *160*, 92–106.

Master, A., Meltzoff, A. N., & Cheryan, S. (2021). Gender stereotypes about interests start early and cause gender disparities in computer science and engineering. *Proceedings of the National Academy of Sciences*, *118*(48), e2100030118.

Master, A., Tang, D., Forsythe, D., Alexander, T. M., Cheryan, S., & Meltzoff, A. N. (2023). Gender equity and motivational readiness for computational thinking in early childhood. *Early Childhood Research Quarterly*, *64*, 242–254.

McClain, C., & Vandermaas-Peeler, M. (2016). Social contexts of development in natural outdoor environments: Children's motor activities, personal challenges and peer interactions at the river and the creek. *Journal of Adventure Education and Outdoor Learning*, *16*(1), 31–48.

Mejias, S., Thompson, N., Sedas, R. M., Rosin, M., Soep, E., Peppler, K., Roche, J., Wong, J. Hurley, M., Bell, P., & Bevan, B. (2021). The trouble with STEAM and why we use it anyway. *Science Education, 105*(2), 209–231.

Meredith, C. C. (2010). Applied learning in teacher education: Developing learning communities among pre-service candidates and urban elementary schools. *Journal of Human Resource and Adult Learning*, 6(2), 80.

Messer, D., Thomas, L., Holliman, A., & Kucirkova, N. (2018). Evaluating the effectiveness of an educational programming intervention on children's mathematics skills, spatial awareness and working memory. *Education and Information Technologies, 23*(6), 2879–2888.

Metz, S. S. (2007). Attracting the engineers of 2020 today. In R. J. Burke, M. C. Mattis, & E. Elgar (Eds.), *Women and minorities in science, technology, engineering and mathematics: Upping the numbers* (pp. 184–209). Edward Elgar.

Miller, E., & Almon, J. (2009). Crisis in the kindergarten: Why children need to play in school. *Alliance for Childhood* (NJ3a). https://files.eric.ed.gov/fulltext/ED504839.pdf

Mohr-Schroeder, M. J., Jackson, C., Miller, M., Walcott, B., Little, D. L., Speler, L., Schooler, W., & Schroeder, D. C. (2014). Developing middle school students' interests in STEM via summer learning experiences: See Blue STEM camp. *School Science and Mathematics, 114*(6), 291–301.

Montessori, M. (1912). *The Montessori method*. Frederick Stokes.

Montie, J. E., Xiang, Z., & Schweinhart, L. J. (2006). Preschool experience in 10 countries: Cognitive and language performance at age 7. *Early Childhood Research Quarterly*, *21*(3), 313–331.

Moomaw, S., & Davis, J. A. (2010). STEM comes to preschool. *YC Young Children, 65*(5), 12.

National Girls Collaborative Project. (2022). *Access to STEM framework*. https://www.milliongirlsmoonshot.org/access-to-stem

National Girls Collaborative Project. (2024). *The state of girls and women in STEM*. https://ngcproject.org/resources/state-girls-and-women-stem

National Research Council. (2009). *Learning science in informal environments: People, places, and pursuits*. National Academies Press.

Ness, D., & Farenga, S. J. (2016). Blocks, bricks, and planks: Relationships between affordance and visuo-spatial constructive play objects. *American Journal of Play, 8*(2), 201–227.

NGSS Lead States. (2013). *Next Generation Science Standards: For states, by states*. National Academies Press.

Nguyen, T. T. K., Ngo, T. P. A., Pham, A. T., Nguyen, D. D., & Cheng, P. H. (2024). Let's play! Transforming STEM education with board games. *Eurasia Journal of Mathematics, Science and Technology Education, 20*(8), Article em2494. https://www.ejmste.com/article/lets-play-transforming-stem-education-with-board-games-14920

Nicholson, S. (1972). The theory of loose parts, an important principle for design methodology. *Studies in Design Education Craft & Technology, 4*(2), 5–14.

Nicolopoulou, A. (1993). Play, cognitive development, and the social world: Piaget, Vygotsky, and beyond. *Human Development, 36*(1), 1–23.

Nicolopoulou, A. (2010). The alarming disappearance of play from early childhood education. *Human Development, 53*(1), 1–4.

NYC Department of Education. (2020). *Computer science for all*. https://infohub.nyced.org/in-our-schools/programs/computer-science-for-all-overview

Ofcom. (2020, February). *Children and parents: Media use and attitudes report 2019*. Ofcom UK. https://www.ofcom.org.uk/__data/assets/pdf_file/0023/190616/children-media-use-attitudes-2019-report.pdf

Oppenheimer, T. (2003). *The flickering mind: The false promise of technology in the classroom, and how learning can be saved*. Random House.

Ornstein, A. C., & Hunkins, F. P. (2018). *Curriculum: Foundations, principles, and issues* (7th ed.). Pearson.

Osborne, J., & Dillon, J. (2007). Research on learning in informal contexts: Advancing the field? *International Journal of Science Education, 29*(12), 1441–1445.

Papadakis, S., & Kalogiannakis, M. (2022). Learning computational thinking development in young children with Bee-Bot educational robotics. In Information Resources Management Association (Ed.), *Research anthology on computational thinking, programming, and robotics in the classroom* (pp. 926–947). IGI Global.

Panagiotopoulos, N. (2024). Capabilities of engineers to build machines with human-like intelligence using artificial intelligence (AI) and machine learning (ML). *Recent Research Advances in Arts and Social Studies, 45*, 123–145.

Papert, S. (1980). *Mindstorms—Children, computers and powerful ideas*. Basic Books.

Papert, S. (1990). *Children, computers and powerful ideas*. Basic Books.

Papert, S. (2000). What's the big idea? Toward a pedagogy of idea power. *IBM Systems Journal, 39*(3–4), 720–729.

Papert, S., & Harel, I. (1991). Situating constructionism. *Constructionism, 36*(2), 1–11.
Paris, D. (2012). Culturally sustaining pedagogy: A needed change in stance, terminology, and practice. *Educational Researcher, 41*(3), 93–97.
Paris, D., & Alim, H. S. (2014). What are we seeking to sustain through culturally sustaining pedagogy? A loving critique forward. *Harvard Educational Review, 84*(1), 85–100. https://doi.org/10.17763/haer.84.1.982l873k2ht16m77
Parten, M. B. (1932). Social participation among pre-school children. *Journal of Abnormal and Social Psychology, 27*(3), 243–269.
Pellegrini, A. D. (2009). *The role of play in human development.* Oxford University Press.
Perez, C. C. (2019). *Invisible women: Data bias in a world designed for men.* Abrams.
Perlman, R. (1976). *Using computer technology to provide a creative learning environment for preschool children.* Logo memo no. 24. MIT Artificial Intelligence Laboratory Publications 260.
Piaget, J. (1953). *The origin of intelligence in children.* International Universities Press.
Piaget, J. (1969). *The mechanisms of perception.* Routledge & Kegan Paul.
Piaget, J. (1973). *To understand is to invent: The future of education.* Grossman.
Pomeroy, S. R. (2012). From STEM to STEAM: Science and art go hand-in-hand. *Scientific American Guest Blog.* https://www.scientificamerican.com/blog/guest-blog/from-stem-to-steam-science-and-the-arts-go-hand-in-hand/
Popovic, G., & Lederman, J. S. (2015). Implications of informal education experiences for mathematics teachers' ability to make connections beyond formal classroom. *School Science and Mathematics, 115*(3), 129–140.
Posner, G. J. (2004). *Analyzing the curriculum* (3rd ed.). McGraw-Hill Education.
Print, M. (1993). *Curriculum development and design* (2nd ed.). Allen & Unwin.
Pruden, S. M., Levine, S. C., & Huttenlocher, J. (2011). Children's spatial thinking: Does talk about the spatial world matter? *Developmental Science, 14*(6), 1417–1430.
Pugh, K. J., & Girod, M. (2007). Science, art, and experience: Constructing a science pedagogy from Dewey's aesthetics. *Journal of Science Teacher Education, 18*(1), 9–27.
Quigley, C. F., Herro, D., & Jamil, F. M. (2017). Developing a conceptual model of STEAM teaching practices. *School Science and Mathematics, 117*(1–2), 1–12.
Rahm, J., & Moore, J. C. (2016). A case study of long-term engagement and identity-in-practice: Insights into the STEM pathways of four underrepresented youths. *Journal of Research in Science Teaching, 53*(5), 768–801. https://doi.org/10.1002/tea.21268
Reed, A. J. S., & Michaud, M. J. (2010). *Goal-driven lesson planning for teaching English to speakers of other languages.* University of Michigan Press.
Reggio Children SRL. (2022). Reggio Emilia approach. Reggio children. https://www.reggiochildren.it/en/reggio-emilia-approach/
Relkin, E., & Strawhacker, A. (2021). Unplugged learning: Recognizing computational thinking in everyday life. In M. Bers (Ed.), *Teaching computational thinking and coding to young children* (pp. 41–62). IGI Global.
Resnick, M. (2006). Computer as paintbrush: Technology, play, and the creative society. In D. Singer, R. Golikoff, & K. Hirsh-Pasek (Eds.), *Play = learning: How play motivates and enhances children's cognitive and social-emotional growth.* Oxford University Press.

Resnick, M., Martin, F., Berg, R., Borovoy, R., Colella, V., Kramer, K., & Silverman, B. (1998, January). Digital manipulatives: New toys to think with. In *Proceedings of the SIGCHI conference on human factors in computing systems* (pp. 281–287). https://dl.acm.org/doi/10.1145/274644.274684

Resnick, M., & Silverman, B. (2005). Some reflections on designing construction kits for kids. In *Proceedings of the 2005 conference on interaction design and children* (pp. 117–122). https://dl.acm.org/doi/10.1145/1109540.1109556

Richards, J. C., & Bohlke, D. (2011). *Creating effective language lessons.* Cambridge University Press.

Robelen, E. W. (2011). STEAM: Experts make case for adding arts to STEM. *Education Week, 31*(13), 8.

Rodriguez, B., Rader, C., & Camp, T. (2016, July). Using student performance to assess CS unplugged activities in a classroom environment. In *Proceedings of the 2016 ACM conference on innovation and technology in computer science education* (pp. 95–100). https://dl.acm.org/doi/10.1145/2899415.2899465

Roese, J. (2021, January 27). COVID-19 exposed the digital divide. Here's how we can close it. *World Economic Forum.* https://www.weforum.org/agenda/2021/01/covid-digital-divide-learning-education.

Root-Bernstein, R. (2011). The art of scientific and technological innovations. *ScienceBlogs.* https://scienceblogs.com/art_of_science_learning/2011/04/11/the-art-of-scientific-and-tech-1

Rubin, K. H. (1986). Play, peers, and social development. In A. W. Gottfried & C. Caldwell Brown (Eds.), *Play interactions: The contribution of play materials and parental involvement to child development* (pp. 163–174). Heath.

Rubin, K. H., Fein, G. C., & Vandenberg, B. (1983). Play. In P. H. Mussen (Ed.), *Handbook of child psychology* (4th ed., pp. 693–774). Wiley.

Salinas-Gonzalez, I., Arreguín-Anderson, M. G., & Alanís, I. (2018). Supporting language: Culturally rich dramatic play. *Teaching Young Children, 11*(2), 4

Sanders, M. (2008). STEM, STEM education, STEMmania. *Technology Teacher, 68*(4), 20–27.

Sarama, J., & Clements, D. H. (2009). *Early childhood mathematics education research: Learning trajectories for young children.* Routledge.

Sarama, J., Lange, A. A., Clements, D. H., & Wolfe, C. B. (2012). The impacts of an early mathematics curriculum on oral language and literacy. *Early Childhood Research Quarterly, 27*(3), 489–502.

Scarlett, W. G., Naudeau, S., Salonius-Pasternak, D., & Ponte, I. (2004). *Children's play.* Sage.

Science Daily. (2014, March 3). *Health benefits from free play confirmed by research.* https://www.sciencedaily.com/releases/2014/03/140303083547.htm

Shah, P. E., Weeks, H. M., Richards, B., & Kaciroti, N. (2018). Early childhood curiosity and kindergarten reading and math academic achievement. *Pediatric Research, 84*(3), 380–386.

Sheridan, K., Halverson, E. R., Litts, B., Brahms, L., Jacobs-Priebe, L., & Owens, T. (2014). Learning in the making: A comparative case study of three makerspaces. *Harvard Educational Review, 84*(4), 505–531.

Shvarts, A., & Bakker, A. (2019). The early history of the scaffolding metaphor: Bernstein, Luria, Vygotsky, and before. *Mind, Culture, and Activity, 26*(1), 4–23.

Singer, D. G., & Singer, J. L. (1990). *The house of make-believe*. Harvard University Press.

Smith, P. K., Takhvar, M., Gore, N., & Vollstedt, R. (1985). Play in young children: Problems of definition, categorisation and measurement. *Early Child Development and Care, 19*(1–2), 25–41.

Smith, P. K., & Vollstedt, R. (1985). On defining play: An empirical study of the relationship between play and various play criteria. *Child Development, 56*(4), 1042–1050.

Sobel, D. (2016). The sky above and the mud below: Lessons from nature preschools and forest kindergartens. In J. Lin, R. Oxford, & T. E. Culham (Eds.), *Toward a spiritual research paradigm: Exploring new ways of knowing, researching and being* (pp. 139–156). Information Age.

Somuncu, B., & Aslan, D. (2022). Effect of coding activities on preschool children's mathematical reasoning skills. *Education and Information Technologies*, *27*(1), 877–890.

ST Office Tokyo. (2019, April 1). Coding will be mandatory in Japan's primary schools from 2020. ST Office Tokyo (ST Office Tokyo—CH). ST Office Tokyo. (2019, April 1). Coding will be mandatory in Japan's primary schools from 2020. ST Office Tokyo (ST Office Tokyo—CH).

Steele, C. M. (1997). A threat in the air: How stereotypes shape intellectual identity and performance. *American Psychologist, 52*(6), 613–629.

Strawhacker, A., & Sullivan, A. (2021). Computational expression: How performance arts support computational thinking in young children. In M. Bers (Ed.), *Teaching computational thinking and coding to young children* (pp. 134–156). IGI Global.

Strawhacker, A. L. (2020). *Biodesign education in early childhood: A design-research study of the tangible CRISPEE technology and learning intervention* [Doctoral dissertation, Tufts University]. Order No. 27962318. ProQuest.

Sullivan, A. (2019). *Breaking the STEM stereotype: Reaching girls in early childhood*. Rowman & Littlefield.

Sullivan, A. (2021). Supporting girls' computational thinking skillsets: Why early exposure is critical to success. In M. Bers (Ed.), *Teaching computational thinking and coding to young children* (pp. 216–235). IGI Global.

Sullivan, A., & Bers, M. U. (2015, March 22). Robotics in the early childhood classroom: Learning outcomes from an eight-week robotics curriculum in pre-kindergarten through second grade. *International Journal of Technology and Design Education, 26*(1), 3–20. https://www.semanticscholar.org/paper/Robotics-in-the-early-childhood-classroom%3A-learning-Sullivan-Bers/49a2e652573112d24150a7b3f83239e502f6dc6c

Sullivan, A., & Bers, M. U. (2017). Dancing robots: Integrating art, music, and robotics in Singapore's early childhood centers. *International Journal of Technology and Design Education, 28*(2), 325–346. https://doi.org/10.1007/s10798-017-9397-0

Sullivan, A., Kazakoff, E. R., & Bers, M. U. (2013). The wheels on the bot go round and round: Robotics curriculum in pre-kindergarten. *Journal of Information Technology Education: Innovations in Practice,* 12, 203–219.

Sullivan, A., & Strawhacker, A. (2021). Screen-free STEAM: Low-cost and hands-on approaches to teaching coding and engineering to young children. In

C. Cohrssen & S. Garvis (Eds.), *Embedding STEAM in early childhood education and care* (pp. 87–113). Palgrave Macmillan.

Sullivan, A., Strawhacker, A., & Bers, M. U. (2017). Dancing, drawing, and dramatic robots: Integrating robotics and the arts to teach foundational STEAM concepts to young children. In M. S. Khine (Ed.), *Robotics in STEM education*. Springer. https://doi.org/10.1007/978-3-319-57786-9_10

Sutton-Smith, B. (2009). *The ambiguity of play*. Harvard University Press.

Szekely, G. (2015). *Play and creativity in art teaching*. Routledge.

The Tech Interactive. (2024). *Computational thinking*. https://www.thetech.org/education/education-resources/lessons-activities/computational-thinking/

Tsai, J. C., Chen, S. Y., Chang, C. Y., & Liu, S. Y. (2020). Element enterprise tycoon: Playing board games to learn chemistry in daily life. *Education Sciences*, *10*(3), Article 48. https://www.researchgate.net/publication/339528160_Element_Enterprise_Tycoon_Playing_Board_Games_to_Learn_Chemistry_in_Daily_Life

Vartiainen, J., & Kumpulainen, K. (2020). Playing with science: Manifestation of scientific play in early science inquiry. *European Early Childhood Education Research Journal*, *28*(4), 490–503.

Vita-Barrull, N., Estrada-Plana, V., March-Llanes, J., Guzmán, N., Fernández-Muñoz, C., Ayesa, R., & Moya-Higueras, J. (2023). Board game-based intervention to improve executive functions and academic skills in rural schools: A randomized controlled trial. *Trends in Neuroscience and Education*, *33*, Article 100216. https://doi.org/10.1016/j.tine.2023.100216

Vosniadou, S. (1994). Capturing and modeling the process of conceptual change. *Learning and Instruction*, *4*(1), 45–69.

Wang, M. T., & Degol, J. L. (2017). Gender gap in science, technology, engineering, and mathematics (STEM): Current knowledge, implications for practice, policy, and future directions. *Educational Psychology Review*, *29*(1), 119–140.

Watson, E. (2020). STEM or STEAM? The critical role of arts in technology education (and the critical role of art in technology). *Irish Journal of Academic Practice*, *8*(1), 8.

White, R. E. (2012). The power of play: A research summary on play and learning. Minnesota Children's Museum. https://mcm.org/wp-content/uploads/2018/06/Research-Summary-1117.pdf

Wing, J. M. (2006). Computational thinking. *Communications of the ACM*, *49*(3), 33–35.

Wolfe, J. (2002). *Learning from the past: Historical voices in early childhood education* (rev. 2nd ed.). Piney Branch Press.

Wolfgang, C. H., Stannard, L. L., & Jones, I. (2001). Block play performance among preschoolers as a predictor of later school achievement in mathematics. *Journal of Research in Childhood Education*, *15*(2), 173–180.

Wood, C. (1997). *Yardsticks: Children in the classroom ages 4-14. A resource for parents and teachers*. Northeast Foundation for Children. https://www.scribd.com/document/210431934/Yardsticks

World Health Organization (WHO). (2019). *Guidelines on physical activity, sedentary behavior and sleep for children under 5 years of age*. World Health Organization. https://www.who.int/publications/i/item/9789241550536

Wyeth, P. (2008). How young children learn to program with sensor, action, and logic blocks. *Journal of the Learning Sciences*, *17*(4), 517–550.

Yakman, G. (2008). STEAM education: An overview of creating a model of integrative education. In *PATT-19 conference proceedings* (pp. 335–358). https://www.researchgate.net/publication/327351326_STEAM_Education_an_overview_of_creating_a_model_of_integrative_education?utm_source=chatgpt.com

Yakman, G. (2010). STEAM: A framework for teaching across the disciplines. *The STEAM Journal, 1*(1), Article 9.

Yakman, G. (2011, September). Introducing teaching STEM as a practical educational framework for Korea. International Seminar on STEAM Education. *Korea Foundation for the Advancement of Science and Creativity,* 1–28.

Zosh, J. M., Gaudreau, C., Golinkoff, R. M., & Hirsh-Pasek, K. (2022). The power of playful learning in the early childhood setting. *YC Young Children, 77*(2), 6–13.

Index

About the Authors

Amanda Sullivan is a researcher, educator, and author who explores the positive impact of exposure to hands-on science, technology, engineering, and mathematics (STEM) during the formative early childhood years. She is passionate about breaking stereotypes and ensuring that all children grow up feeling welcome in STEM. Dr. Sullivan is a senior researcher at the National Girls Collaborative Project (NGCP), a nonprofit organization with the vision of creating STEM experiences that are as diverse as the world we live in. She is the author of the book *Breaking the STEM Stereotype: Reaching Girls in Early Childhood* and co-creator of the ScratchJr Coding Cards: Creative Coding Activities. Dr. Sullivan's work has been featured in *GeekWire, WIRED* magazine, the *New York Times*, the *Boston Globe*, and more. She holds a master's and PhD in child development from Tufts University and a bachelor's degree in psychology and drama from Bennington College. Dr. Sullivan is the proud mom of two curious and energetic young children who inspire her passion for play-based learning.

Amanda Strawhacker is an early childhood author and educator whose research in school curriculum and product design focuses on introducing children to novel STEAM fields in playful, developmentally appropriate ways. She is the STEAM coordinator at Schechter Boston school in Massachusetts and has contributed to the development of commercially available educational STEAM products (including the KIBO robotics kit, the ScratchJr programming app, and others). Dr. Strawhacker is a speaker and writer whose work has been disseminated through outlets like TEDx@BeaconStreet. She holds a master's and PhD in child study and human development, and a bachelor's degree in anthropology from Tufts University, and learns even more about playful learning every day from her fierce and fun-loving young daughter.